Gillian Armstrong

Gillian Armstrong

Popular, Sensual and Ethical Cinema

Julia Erhart

EDINBURGH
University Press

Edinburgh University Press is one of the leading university presses in the UK. We publish academic books and journals in our selected subject areas across the humanities and social sciences, combining cutting-edge scholarship with high editorial and production values to produce academic works of lasting importance. For more information visit our website: edinburghuniversitypress.com

We are committed to making research available to a wide audience and are pleased to be publishing Platinum Open Access editions of the ebooks in this series.

Edinburgh University Press Ltd
The Tun – Holyrood Road
12(2f) Jackson's Entry
Edinburgh EH8 8PJ

Typeset in 12/14 Arno and Myriad by
IDSUK (DataConnection) Ltd, and
printed and bound by CPI Group (UK) Ltd, Croydon, CR0 4YY

A CIP record for this book is available from the British Library

ISBN 978 1 4744 4051 6 (hardback)
ISBN 978 1 4744 3432 4 (paperback)
ISBN 978 1 4744 3433 1 (webready PDF)
ISBN 978 1 4744 3434 8 (epub)

Contents

Figures

Acknowledgements

Preliminary research and writing for this book began at a very sad time when my mother's health was precipitously declining. That year, I made the thirty-hour-long trip between Adelaide, Australia and my mother's home in Portland, Maine five times. Each time, Gillian Armstrong's movies accompanied me on my laptop; they became my travelling companions. Since then, I have spent many more hours 'with' Armstrong's remarkable movies. My first thanks go to her for making them.

I am grateful to series editors Lucy Bolton and Richard Rushton for supporting the idea for a book about Armstrong, encouraging me, and providing excellent feedback along the way. I thank the anonymous 'Reader A' of my initial proposal, who nudged me in the direction of the feminist frameworks which ultimately became indispensable. At Edinburgh, Gillian Leslie and Richard Strachan were helpful shepherding the book from commissioning to copy-editing.

This book benefited from various presentation opportunities as it was being written. *Doing Women's Film and Television History* in Southampton in 2018, *Society for Cinema and Media Studies* in Seattle in 2019, and *Contemporary Women's Cinema and Media: Aesthetics, Identities, and Imaginaries* at *Roma Tre* in 2019 provided chances to connect with friendly scholars and trial some of these ideas.

In Australia, thanks are owed to friends and colleagues who watched movies, read drafts, and/or were there to listen: Helen Carter, Therese Davis, Nicholas Godfrey, Amy Matthews, Sarah

Peters, Will Peterson, and Claire Whitley. In the Flinders library, research support staff provided much needed assistance tracking down interviews with Armstrong. To those who granted or helped me secure permission to reprint photographs, Ewen Campbell, Debi Enker, Carolyn Johns, Sue Mathews, and Heather O'Brien at Entertainment Media, thank you.

To Jackson and Kit: biggest thanks for your never-ending sarcasm and for being the kinds of teenagers that are fun to hang around with. There, I said it.

Finally, to Susan. There's no way I could have written this without you. Thank you, always.

Introduction

Four minutes into Gillian Armstrong's last major film, *Women He's Undressed* (2015), costume designer Orry-Kelly delivers an uninterrupted monologue describing the early days in his friendship with Archie Leach/Cary Grant in the years when they first arrived in New York City, before either became famous. Kelly delivers the monologue while seated in a red rowboat on the back of which 'Kiama' is painted, the name of the small seaside Australian town where Orry was born. Presented with conviction, the speech introduces key themes of Orry's courage as a gay man living in Hollywood in the 1930s when gayness was unacceptable, and the story of his escape from small-town Australia. Towards the end of this monologue, Orry picks up the oars and begins to row, but the boat remains motionless because it is on a wooden stage set. Orry, it would seem, isn't going anywhere.

Let me turn to a scene from a film from the very beginning of Armstrong's working life. The third and final film made by Armstrong while a student at Swinburne art school, the eight-minute long experimental film *The Roof Needs Mowing* (1971) relies (like *Women He's Undressed*) on absurdist and surreal imagery to communicate with audiences. The opening shots show family members silently seated around a breakfast table, vying for the radio. The footage speeds up, with the 'mother' and adult 'children' arriving and departing in fast motion while the 'father' remains at the centre of the frame, continuing in regular motion to eat and read the paper. He utters what seems a non sequitur: 'I've always had this dream of running away and joining the circus.'[1] For the remainder of the short, the man stays stationary in an unmoving rowboat while others speed past in different boats, including the movie's 'mother' and a group of girls in Brownie uniforms. Exactly as in *Women He's Undressed*, the man's boat doesn't move and at the end of *The Roof Needs Mowing* the camera pulls back to show the boat is located awkwardly in a small, above-ground swimming pool.[2]

Separated by nearly forty-five years, the two scenes contain a number of formal similarities, including the placement and movements of the actors in the frame, their physical appearance as forty-something white men dressed in business suits, and the fact that both are seated in immobilised rowboats. In both movies, the rowboat scenes are framing devices bookending their respective narratives, and in both movies the camera draws back to reveal – as a kind of visual gag – a boat going nowhere. Common to both movies are characteristics that distinguish them from Armstrong's work as a whole: both *Women He's Undressed* and *The Roof Needs Mowing* are formally experimental, relatively uninvested in conventional systems of commercial distribution, and focused mainly on the position of men rather than women.

In spite of their differences from Armstrong's other movies, the existential and emotional themes these two movies exhibit – characters caught in claustrophobic settings, individuals who are imprisoned or oppressed because of circumstances, the toxicity of stasis, and the imagined pleasure offered by escape, if/when it arrives – are abiding and prevalent across the whole of Armstrong's oeuvre from beginning to end, in nearly all of Armstrong's dramas and documentaries, regardless of production circumstances or location of production. These themes are seen in *My Brilliant Career* and *Mrs. Soffel*, in *High Tide* and *The Last Days of Chez Nous*, in *Starstruck* and *Oscar and Lucinda*; we see them in Armstrong's five-part series, *The Story of Kerry, Josie and Diana*.

All of Armstrong's films communicate in richly rendered detail the specific textures, noises, and colours of the locations where their featured protagonists live and die; they do this via cinematography, costuming, *mise-en-scène*, editing, scripting, and sound design. All of them depict complex characters in challenging and often unusual circumstances; nearly all tell stories of journey and/or escape. Sybylla Melvyn, Kate Soffel, Lucinda Leplastrier, Jackie Mullens, Josephine March, Lilli, Beth, Kerry, Diana, and Josie *all* seek to depart stifling domestic circumstances; the journeys that each of these undertakes form the basis of the stories which Armstrong tells.

When she directed *My Brilliant Career* in 1979, Gillian Armstrong became the first Australian woman to make a feature film in Australia in over forty years.[3] In the second decade of the twenty-first century she is a commercially successful director of over eighteen feature films and documentaries and an important, early example of a woman director connecting with mass audiences who has crafted an authorial image that is powerful and unique. Armstrong has built an illustrious career around commercial, popular genre films, with multiple Australian productions and international co-productions to her name, and smaller-scale low-budget Australian dramas; she has a well-earned reputation as an innovator in documentary, with her longitudinal series about three girls growing up in South Australia and her two experimental biographical documentaries. Armstrong's movies are unique in their aesthetic expression and in the ethical relationships that they depict. Both Armstrong the director and her films have been framed through the language of gender inclusivity, due to her frequent foregrounding of female characters and themes of interest to women audiences, and due to her getting started at a time of crippling disadvantage for women wanting a career in screen.

This book claims that Armstrong is a major director in Australian and international cinemas worthy of scrutiny and celebration and an innovator in film language across multiple industrial and aesthetic spaces. A prime motivator for the book is my belief that Armstrong has not received the recognition she deserves; while there is a literature responding to single films of hers as they were released, to date there has been just one scholarly monograph published about this important director, Felicity Collins's excellent *The Films of Gillian Armstrong* (1999).[4]

Collins's book fills many gaps for scholars and fans and engages deeply with Armstrong's vision of cinema, examining the forms and themes that make a 'Gillian Armstrong film'. But since Collins's book, Armstrong has produced five new features (two transnationally produced period features, two experimental biographical documentaries, and her final installation in the long-form documentary series *The Story of Kerry, Josie and Diana*). Armstrong's short films have never received much attention and aspects of her filmmaking have not been positioned as prominently as they ought to be. Armstrong's participation in an oral history project at the Australian National Film and Sound Archive has never to my knowledge been utilised; this resource provides an important insight into Armstrong's own thoughts and reflections, and readers will see it is integral to this book. Getting her start at the end of the 1960s and still active in social media spaces, Armstrong's career stretches across a production terrain that is remarkable for its historical breadth; her ability to negotiate across these periods is truly trailblazing. There is new urgency for understanding the contributions of women media practitioners brought about by political movements like #MeToo and #Time's Up. Quite simply, there is a burgeoning literature on women filmmakers and Armstrong ought to be more visible in it.

What has also transpired in the twenty years since Collins's publication is that film studies – and feminist film studies in particular – has ventured into new scholarly terrains and consolidated new philosophical partnerships, with which much of Armstrong's work is interestingly entangled. Where once there existed but one lens through which to examine feminist practice – the language of psychoanalysis – feminism and film studies since the year 2000 have broadened to include issues of ethics, affect, the sensorial, the place of the popular in media consumption, and new industrial histories of women creative practitioners. There is now a rich methodological terrain across which women's media engagements potentially stretch. With a kind of uncanny mirroring that is born of their shared historical co-location, Armstrong's work is complexly imbricated in many of these scholarly debates. As I hope to show, Armstrong has much to tell us about ethical and affective practice, and about the relevance of popular genres. A fuller road map for these offerings will come towards the end of this introduction.

So where to begin? Collins rightly notes that preoccupations and perspectives that appear throughout Armstrong's life's work are present in her early shorts (1999: 8). Armstrong's shorts have not, as stated, been much discussed. I am not aware of any extended scholarly writing about them, in spite of their location at the start of Armstrong's career and potential to shed light on Armstrong's early influences and concerns, in spite of the diversity they exhibit in theme and genre, and in spite of the otherwise demonstrably high regard within Australian screen studies and culture for short films as a film genre and an art form. In this introduction, I explore these movies as harbingers of things to come. Let us have a look at what is there at the very start.

Always Armstrong: form and style

At the beginning of this introduction I drew attention to Armstrong's interest in experimental techniques via a discussion of her 1971 Swinburne graduation film. There is evidence that Armstrong was nurturing these interests even earlier than 1971. *Old Man and Dog* (1970), made at Swinburne before *The Roof Needs Mowing*, contains the bare bones of a story which is retold three times in succession, with slight differences each time. With each retelling the shots become shorter, the camera work more disorienting, and the editing quicker. In the first sketch, an older man enters and exits a shop while a medium-size black dog waits outside; both the man and the dog make their way down the sidewalk and to a sports stadium, where the man takes a seat in the top row. There are ellipses in the joining of the shots, but each action is shown more or less from beginning to end within each shot. The pace of the actions is slow as if to mimic the elderly man's pace, and the camera movement is kept to a minimum. A still camera depicts a train passing fully through the frame in a long shot, and a final sequence of five shots concludes the sketch and shows the man riding a bike across the sports pitch. In the second iteration, the man again enters the shop while the dog waits, only this time a close-up on the man's hands is shown. There are other subtle differences: as the man ascends the stadium, he is shot from the back, and a close-up of the man's hands feeding sausage to the dog is included. As before, the train goes by but in this second iteration the camera is positioned closer to the train and the shot duration is more clipped. In the third and final iteration the actions become even more discontinuous, the cutting even more rapid, and the framing more disorienting. There are many extreme close-ups and careening movements.

Although Armstrong would go on to earn a reputation as a maker of realist fiction films and observational documentaries and her filmmaking would never again be so formally experimental, a central departure point for this book is the centrality of film form to Armstrong's creative expression and her commitment to using the full range of cinema's aesthetic potential to communicate a diversity of emotional states. With this early film, Armstrong's experimentation with the radical potential of her newly discovered medium is fully on display; there is playfulness, pleasure, and joy in her investigation of how escalated editing and dramatised framing and cinematography can alter audience perceptions of space, time, and character.

I am framing *Old Man and Dog* as a privileged viewpoint on to Armstrong's young creative self and through this, inviting readers to learn more about how this burgeoning interest goes on to inform Armstrong's future filmmaking. *Old Man and Dog* is the moment when we can see Armstrong becoming aware of how much cinema could say and committed to exploring all it was able to offer. How this experiment threads through her subsequent movie making, will be demonstrated throughout this book.

At the Australian Film and Television School

When Armstrong enrolled at the newly founded Australian Film and Television School (AFTS), she gained the opportunity to add a raft of storytelling knowledge and skills to her cinematic toolkit. The first film Armstrong made at AFTS, *One Hundred a Day* (1973), was a 1930s-set period film about Leilia (Rosalie Fletcher), a young woman worker in a shoe factory, who obtains an abortion. The film was adapted from a chapter in the novel *How Beautiful Are Thy Feet* by Australian writer Alan Marshall ([1949] 1972). It captured the sympathetic, social realist flavour of the book and much of Marshall's dialogue and incorporated a selection of images, approach to casting, costuming, and performance which in hindsight we might want to call 'signature' Armstrong.

The black-and-white film opens with a brief tracking shot showing the busy, noisy factory locale. Following the camera's movement behind heavy machinery, there is a montage sequence of the mechanical fast-moving factory equipment. Comprised of almost twenty shots of rhythmically moving shoemaking machines forcefully and repetitiously cutting, punching, and polishing the raw leather and shoe materials, the sequence is long (twenty seconds in duration) and emphasises the dehumanising machine-like quality of life in the factory for the mostly female workforce. The accompanying soundtrack is loud, clanging and drawn from the noisy factory floor, emphasising the repetitious-ness of the work and how it impedes regular human intercourse (i.e. talking). Although it is a bustling space, the work environment is not one of happy productivity but of drudgery and toil, and shots of machinery contrast sharply with extreme close-ups of Leilia's expressive, apprehensive face, often beaded with sweat from the hard factory labour and from emotional anxiety. Shots in the factory and subsequently at the office of the abortion provider focus concertedly on the human face.

In the first instance, Armstrong's experience making this film was one of deep appreciation for the support extended by the film school; after working as an assistant director in the fledging Australian film industry, Armstrong recognised what a privilege it was to be supported to work under quasi-professional conditions, with professional actors, editors, cinematographers, and make-up artists. While at AFTS, students enjoyed access to professional-quality dubbing studios and assistance with location scouting. In the case of *One Hundred a Day*, Storry Walton (then head of AFTS) assisted by identifying the real working shoe factory where sewing machines were still in use and brokered the arrangement for Armstrong to shoot there (Shirley 2011). Pre-production involved AFTS flying Armstrong to meet with Marshall to discuss adapting a chapter for her film (Shirley 2011).

Rising to the challenge of creating a period-set film while still a student (even with the support of the School), Armstrong carried out extensive research and was fastidious in her attention to detail. She studied 1930s photos, sought young actors with face shapes suited to the time, and even melted wax to form the young women's mascara, emulating historical make-up techniques (Shirley 2011). On set, Armstrong learned to stay true to the vision of what she wanted to achieve, even when this meant reshooting scenes numerous times. The result of these efforts was a much-lauded film that became one of the top four nominated films at the Sydney film festival short film category that year, and which resulted in Armstrong's director of photography (Ross King) and editor (David Stiven) winning awards. *One Hundred a Day* became Armstrong's industry calling card after graduation and reconfirmed Armstrong's interest – on display in *The Roof* – in themes of claustrophobia and confinement.

There are many ways *One Hundred a Day* anticipates aesthetic foci and thematic concerns that would come to be seen in numerous future films of Armstrong. Shots of Leilia and her friends at the factory and the abortion clinic foretell Armstrong's interest in women characters and communities. The deployment of close-ups on the women's faces and their comments about working life herald both a burgeoning ability to use visual communication to express internal emotions and her dexterity to observe, without judgement, people performing in challenging situations. The film furthermore confirms an ability that Armstrong would rely on over her career's course, which was the aptitude to conduct research for a project set in an entirely different era, and oversee the mobilising of props, costuming, set components, and make-up associated with it. Armstrong would eventually draw upon these skills and competencies during the making of practically all of her popular genre films, discussed in Chapters 2 and 3 of this book.

Satdee Night (1973)

Armstrong's second AFTS production was the documentary-drama hybrid short *Satdee Nite*. If *One Hundred a Day* showed off Armstrong's skills in pre-production and period design, *Satdee Night* was an experiment in the expressive potential of under-production: much of the film is shot handheld, in contemporary domestic settings, and there appears to be some improvisation in the dialogue. The first three-fifths of the movie focus on the ordinary, self-care rituals of the lead character, Stuart, as he wakes, rises, cleans house, grooms himself, and eats in preparation for a night out. These sections are shot entirely in the interior of a house in a suburban Sydney location, the camera movement is (as said) largely handheld, and there is no extra-diegetic music. The camera stays in close proximity with the protagonist – played by Armstrong's real housemate Stuart Campbell – as he goes about his preparations. He is heard joyously singing while the focus is on intimate bodily actions: his shaving around his beard and forehead, application of deodorant, putting on of clothes, and lacing up of shoes. None of the activities are rushed and most are depicted in real time. Eventually, Stuart stops off at another house for a meal, where casual seemingly unscripted banter is heard; Stuart leaves for the town hall in Glebe, the inner-city Sydney suburb where the dance takes place. While at the dance, the camerawork grows more frenetic, capturing non-professional community members and Stuart as he tries to join in. Shots centre him in frame, looking confused, surreptitiously drinking, staring into the camera, overwhelmed. He attempts to sit and ends up falling to the floor, inebriated.

The motivation for this film was the School's stipulation that all students should gain experience in documentary; typically, this meant that the students' second film would be in that form. In spite of the fact she would go on to build a strong reputation as a director of documentaries, Armstrong at this time negotiated with the head of AFTS to create a different hybrid project applying documentary skills and storytelling to what would essentially be a dramatised story. Actors Armstrong sourced included non-professional members of the gay community and her flatmate, Stuart Campbell. According to Armstrong, the genesis of the story was Stuart's real-life experience of preparing to attend a community dance, falling asleep, and waking up the next morning (having largely missed the event).

In formal terms, *Satdee Night*'s mix of documentary and dramatic conventions was innovative, in that a good deal of the film's grammar drew from observational documentary, but with a story that was pre-scripted. Other aspects positioned the film as a dramatised documentary; this included the movie's concluding titles, 'as told to Merran Fuller, Robyn and Wolf Kress, Judy Woodroffe, Gerrard Allen and Doug Anders by Stuart Campbell'. The formal hybridity displayed by *Satdee Night* signalled an interest in the rhetorics of documentary expression which would become apparent over the course of Armstrong's five-part South Australian documentary series and in her two experimental biographical documentaries. This series is discussed in Chapter 5 and the biographical documentaries are explored in Chapter 4.

What is also notable about the movie is the trust that Armstrong needed to secure with the gay community at the time. In comparison with *One Hundred a Day*, *Satdee Nite* drew considerably fewer accolades from the industry, however there is evidence that the movie achieved a positive reception in queer communities (perhaps due to the paucity of movies which dealt with the pressures of being gay in 1973) and has had a life in LGBTQ film festivals around the world.[5] Armstrong has claimed that hers was the first largely straight crew to be allowed in the intimate space of the community dance hall (Shirley 2011); visuals appear to confirm that the dance sequence was largely shot on location, as claimed. Accomplishing this would have required negotiation on Armstrong's part with a community she was not personally affiliated with and anticipates the pre-production negotiations undertaken by Armstrong for *The Story of Kerry, Josie and Diana*. The completion of this film indicates Armstrong's ability to generate trust with her documentary subjects. A discussion about these processes is included in Chapter 5.

Gretel (1973)

For her third and final AFTS film, Armstrong once again made use of a short story written by an Australian writer, Hal Porter, in 1963, about an Australian man living overseas who is called back to Australia following his mother's death (1963). *Gretel's* time frame was complex; it shuttled between past and present and included extended sequences of backwards-looking reverie.[6] True to Porter's story, the film begins with a tracking shot inside a Greek bar that appears to be closing for the night. Sitting and playing cards with a drag queen, a middle-aged Australian man receives a note informing him to return home. The man makes his way to his childhood home for the funeral and reunification with his sister. The sound of children's singing bridges to a scene from the man's past when he was a twelve- or thirteen-year-old boy growing up at the very same house. Matthew suffers a broken arm and while semi-content to nibble biscuits by the fire with his head in a book, close-ups of his face, while his mother's aimless patter is heard in the background, indicate a brewing spirit of rebelliousness. Lurching shots of the green canopy overhead indicate there is more going on than the story lets on, and one day he finally contravenes the order not to visit the girl in the room at the other end of the house. The encounter between Matthew and Gretel is halting and rigid but the length of respective takes of Matthew staring straight into the camera at Gretel and Gretel staring straight back at Matthew seem full of promise and wonder, at a moment and in a world where both children are essentially captive to their respective parents' wishes. The final present-day-set scene reveals Gretel – afflicted with a life-long unidentified mental illness – never managed to escape, but spent her life confined to a tower in a nearby home, dressed with the same jewellery and holding the very same doll as when Matthew first met her.

Though Armstrong's description of her experience making Gretel is not 100 per cent positive (for example, she has claimed that she found some aspects of the script melodramatic and there were challenges in crew (Shirley 2011)), the film went on to screen in the shorts programme at the Sydney Film Festival. Story themes, of claustrophobia and confinement and the ill effects of domination and oppression, particularly on women, anticipate what would be evidenced in many feature films to come.

After AFTS

Adapted from the short story 'Old Mrs. Bilson' by Alan Marshall, *The Singer and the Dancer* (1977) is the final film that Armstrong made before she broke into the feature film market. *The Singer and the Dancer* refers to the respective aspirations of two white women in country Australia, both of whom suffer unhappy home lives, and who discover each other by chance and become friends. The family members of both women are depicted as utterly lacking in sympathy and understanding and lie to them outright. Australian character actor Ruth Cracknell plays Mrs Bilson, the older adoptive mother of a mean-spirited adult daughter, who treats her aging mother as if she were a child. In her daughter's patronising care, Mrs Bilson performs the part of an 'elderly' woman. She is unresponsive, catatonic and moves stiffly; however, the moment her daughter disappears from view, Mrs Bilson undergoes a radical transformation. She irreverently props her feet up on the dashboard of the car, lights up a cigarette, and gallivants across the countryside, bringing a new approach to liberation and aging that remains fresh and original even forty years later (aided by Cracknell's considerable talent as a comedic actor; Cracknell went on to have a lead role in the ten-year-long Australian television hit sitcom *Mother and Son*). Charlie (Elisabeth Crosby) is the film's other female lead who, with her boyfriend, opts to leave suburban Glebe and move to the country for a fresh start. While Charlie is young and optimistic, the boyfriend is petulant and condescending, and he eventually cheats on Charlie with another woman.

Over time, the unlikely friendship between Charlie and Mrs Bilson has a chance to blossom. Scenes show them playfully interacting by the side of a creek and around the farm hillside. Scenes of their socialising together are followed by scenes of them with family members, contrasting their friendship with the worsening conditions for each woman with their primary relationships. Parallels develop when it is revealed that the husband/boyfriend of both the younger and the older women engaged in an affair; here Armstrong experiments with flashbacks and cross-cutting between different historical time frames to tell the two stories in parallel. A final shot shows the younger woman returning to her home, as if to acquiesce to the fate of living with her unfaithful man.

In visual and thematic terms, the film makes use of a number of recurring motifs: shots of women behind windows, watching silently as if imprisoned, with the face part-way hidden behind a window frame; graphic matching shots of the two women friends, establishing a visual grammar of the similarity of their physical positions and thus suggesting their comradery; slow, seemingly handheld tracking shots, often of aspects of Australian farming country; the recurrence of husbands' and boyfriends' lack of fidelity across different historical moments; the benefits of the journey and physical escape; and the possibilities of women's fulfilment from other women, rather than husbands or family members.

The Singer and the Dancer is the first of two films directed by Armstrong where the gender of one of the main characters was changed from male to female (the second was *High Tide*). Where Marshall's original story featured two young male mates who befriend an older lady, Armstrong replaced the young men with the female character, Charlie; in doing this she was able to include in her film version qualities of women's friendship and opportunities for feminist critique of the shared experiences of infidelity and domestic imprisonment, which do not feature in the original story. The film anticipates a number of themes that will become significant across Armstrong's career; these include an interest in the social underdog, the significance of telling stories from women's perspectives, the importance of women's friendships and communities, and the complexity of women's allegiances to each other. These themes will be taken up repeatedly and with surgical precision in many of Armstrong's best-known fiction films and documentaries, including *High Tide*, *Little Women*, *The Last Days of Chez Nous*, and in her five-part documentary series *The Story of Kerry, Josie and Diana*.

Starting points

The idea for this book was born of the twin desires to firstly reintroduce current-day audiences to Armstrong and her work who otherwise might not be aware of it. *My Brilliant Career* premiered over forty years ago and while *Little Women* received some mention with the release of the 2019 remake, it's unlikely that audiences will know the full breadth of her body of work. Secondly, the idea for the book grew out of my own personal commitment to take seriously the contributions of feminist practitioners and their augmenting and enrichment of the methodologies and fields of enquiries of feminist film scholarship. The increased prevalence of terms like 'practice-led theory' and 'practice-based research' in higher education/the tertiary sector indicate the increasing overlap, interrelatedness, and inter-dependence of approaches that were once held separate, to everybody's detriment.

Some time ago I presented a paper called 'Practice Makes Theory Perfect', in which I argued that women practitioners were leaps and bounds ahead of feminist media researchers in their imaginative proposals for creative solutions to issues of women's erasure from the historical record; that paper went on to become part of a book about women's film practice and historical representation (Erhart 2018). This new book is obviously a different project, but my conviction about the need to take seriously the contributions of filmmakers, and to decipher how their work proposes solutions to thorny conceptual problems, has not attenuated. I hope the philosophical and conceptual frames this book provides may be useful for reading and appreciating Armstrong's work; I *know* Armstrong has everything to teach us through her films about these matters.

Armstrong's work has not yet been analysed through the film-philosophical lenses which this book provides. This book aims to bring Armstrong's work into dialogue with new lines of enquiry and probe her unique engagement with a broader set of concerns about authorship, genre and popular cinema, the sensorial, and ethics. It explores what kind of a film author Armstrong is and what her approach has to offer other women directors, how she has negotiated the world of popular genre films, and how her movies address and affect audiences.

The methodologies employed in this book are mixed. Research involved identifying recurring aesthetic and conceptual themes across Armstrong's works as well as canvassing English-language critical reviews of Armstrong and other sources (such as oral histories). As an early director in a sexist industry that has been openly hostile to women at times, Armstrong's negotiation of production circumstances is of interest; this is canvassed in Chapter 1.

This book comprises five main chapters, each of which puts Armstrong's movies into conversation with a body of screen theories and ideas with the aim of highlighting what makes Armstrong's films and/or approach to filmmaking unique. None of the theoretical clusters are exclusively of interest to feminist scholars, though in each case feminist scholars have productively engaged with and contoured the terms of the respective discussion. The chapters outline this engagement, in terms of how it matters for our understanding of Armstrong. The intention of the book overall is to be reciprocal in the handling of theories and practices and to demonstrate how Armstrong's movies illuminate certain conceptual terrains, and how these concepts in turn bring new understanding to Armstrong's film practice.

Outlining of chapters

Chapter 1, 'An authorial cinema', tracks the changing and frequently contradictory ways Armstrong has been visible as an author over the course of her career and identifies the discursive dimensions within which her career as an Australian woman filmmaker became possible. The chapter establishes that Armstrong's authorship is multivalent and has different meanings in different contexts. By considering journalistic and critical reviews of Armstrong and her work and interviews with Armstrong, the chapter explores key themes in her authorship and how Armstrong has at times reconfigured these to suit her own professional needs. The chapter highlights the conditions and contexts in which Armstrong has worked and paints a portrait of the survival strategies employed by Armstrong over the course of this long period.

Chapter 2, 'A popular, commercial cinema', is the first of two chapters exploring Armstrong's achievements within the sometimes aesthetically and socially conservative space of popular genre movies. Armstrong has never kept secret the fact that she always wanted to reach a wide audience; for these reasons I have allowed ample space for exploring Armstrong's storytelling innovations in this area. This chapter considers in chronological order Armstrong's two Hollywood films and two transnational productions, *Mrs. Soffel* and *Little Women* and *Charlotte Gray* and *Death Defying Acts*. All of these films rely on period film conventions, tell their stories from the perspective of a dynamic leading female protagonist, and offer innovative contributions to ideas about women's experience and agency. The chapter is attentive to production circumstances and the social contexts in which the movies were made.

Chapter 3, 'An Australian genre cinema' extends Chapter 2's concerns to explore how Armstrong's domestically produced popular movies reshape generic components to bring a feminist point of view to the recounting of recent and colonial-era Australian histories. The chapter examines how generic elements in Armstrong's two Australian-set period movies dovetail with gender and race to render an affecting history, and how the pro-queer, youth-oriented movie *Starstruck* blends themes from the backstage musical with Australian elements. As I will explain, Armstrong's career took shape in the shadow of the Australian film revival and the relationship between the two has been closely intertwined ever since. For these reasons, it seemed important to include a chapter focusing exclusively on Armstrong's Australian genre films.

Chapter 4, 'A sensual cinema', is an examination of the mostly non-verbal aspects of Armstrong's movies – such as framing, design, and colour elements, the impression of tactility, taste, and smell – and the place of such elements in Armstrong's movies. The chapter considers how Armstrong herself values such qualities and prioritises them via her production choices. The chapter explores what impact and meaning these aesthetic choices are able to communicate to audiences. The chapter focuses principally on Armstrong's realist drama, *The Last Days of Chez Nous*, and her two most recent experimental documentaries, *Unfolding Florence* and *Women He's Undressed*.

'An ethical cinema' is the title of Chapter 5, which considers the ethical concerns that Armstrong's dramatic feature films and documentaries explore. The chapter reviews relevant philosophical discussions about ethical challenges and opportunities that are specific to cinema. The chapter draws the conclusion that

Armstrong contributes to ethical cinematic discourse, invites new forms of audience engagement, and sets a representational model for new ethical relations between characters. The chapter engages closely with *High Tide* and Armstrong's five-part documentary series, *The Story of Kerry, Josie and Diana*.

To conclude: the contents of the five chapters were arrived at after comprehensive viewing and re-viewing of Armstrong's movies; reading, re-reading, listening, and re-listening to print and recorded interviews with Armstrong; and a thorough absorption of scholarly and journalistic literature. The goal was to discover how best to present Armstrong's innovations. As for choosing which films to discuss where: in the interests of providing readers unfamiliar with Armstrong the optimum chance to engage with her work, early on I made a decision to try to include all of Armstrong's feature films, with as little repetition as possible between chapters. The single feature-length film of Armstrong's which is mentioned but which does not receive an extensive discussion is *Fires Within*, on account of Armstrong's strong disassociation from it.[7]

Given the demonstrated thematic and stylistic consistency across Armstrong's work, not surprisingly many of her movies display elements that are potentially of relevance within more than one chapter. Many of her movies could easily have been discussed at length within two or three chapters. In the long run, decisions about where to position the movies had to be made; for this I used a combination of factors, including movie exemplariness and a commitment to giving equal attention across all the movies. Thus, the movies which Chapter 2 focuses on (*Mrs. Soffel, Little Women, Charlotte Gray, Death Defying Acts*) differ from those canvassed in Chapter 3 (*My Brilliant Career, Oscar and Lucinda, Starstruck*); the movies which Chapter 4 largely concentrates on (*The Last Days of Chez Nous, Women He's Undressed, Unfolding Florence: The Many Lives of Florence Broadhurst*) are different from those discussed in prior chapters; the same is true for Chapter 5 (which largely concentrates on *High Tide* and *The Story of Kerry, Josie and Diana*).

Notes

1 Armstrong has described her father as an amateur photographer who gave up his artwork to become a real estate salesman and claimed that the film's central character was loosely based on him (Shirley 2011).

2 Armstrong received support from the Heinz company in the form of thirty-seven giant cans of baked beans that appear in one of the scenes. Heinz even came over and took press photos but didn't end up using them (Shirley 2011).

3 Although it is often said that *My Brilliant Career* is the 'first feature' directed in Australia by a woman since (the now-lost) *Two Minutes of Silence* (1933, dir. Paulette McDonagh), *The Golden Cage* (1975), directed in Australia by a Turkish woman, Ayten Kuyululu, actually appeared four years prior to Armstrong's film.

4 And as Armstrong has become older, a handful of summarising scholarly essays have emerged. See Donald (2017); Weinstein (2013).

5 The film has enjoyed screenings at the Sydney *Queer Screen* festival over the years and was exhibited with other queer-themed movies in programmes offered by the Sydney Co-op (Peach 2005: 202). *Satdee Night* is also currently available via Bent TV Archive, <https://www.youtube.com/watch?v=kkYFfit3Z6E> (last accessed 7 April 2020).

6 There were practical challenges: the person who was responsible for the art department became sick and Armstrong had to take on that role (Shirley 2011).

7 Armstrong has referred to this film as both a 'sad nightmare' and a production 'turkey'. She has discussed her attempts to have her name removed from the film. See Shirley (2011).

1

An authorial cinema

Film authorship or auteurism, as the idea that the director is the main meaning-maker of a movie, has cast a long shadow over the discourse of film studies for most of the second half of the twentieth century. Countless books and university courses have promised to reveal authorial 'signatures' across a director's body of work. While authorship retains traction in smaller-budget cinemas where the director uncontrovertibly exerts creative control, its relevance for high-end commercial cinema – where decision-making is done by production companies and final cuts often determined by test audiences – is increasingly questionable. The irony of the fact that the notion of the author is becoming less relevant precisely when interest in women authors has taken off, has been pointed out (Tasker 2010). Nonetheless feminist media scholars are making important contributions to current-day un-derstandings of film authorship and the first two decades of the twenty-first century have seen an outpouring of scholarly interest in women film creatives, manifested in new book series, journals, conferences, networks, and sole-authored monographs (Hastie 2007; Stamp 2015; Gaines 2018).[1] Researchers are tracking the opportunities and achievements of women media workers within different national and historical spaces, including contemporary Hollywood and in cinemas from Brazil, Italy, Palestine, Indonesia, Spain, and Canada, and focusing on women's negotiation of industrial aspects, including their positioning in prestige venues like film festivals (White 2015). In popular spheres, authorship is a powerful notion for television and movie fans whose entertainment choices are often organised around the work of a particular director or show runner and who speak knowledge- ably and enthusiastically of favoured movie directors and show runners. In concert with concerns brought to the fore by the #MeToo movement, interest in the political dimension of women's authorship has stepped up and become visible through such social media sites as 'Shit People Say To Women Directors'.

Over the course of more than forty years in the industry, Gillian Armstrong has been one of Australia's most significant and visible film authors. Armstrong's personal biography and the story of her acquisition of film language and training has been described (Collins 1999; Shirley 2011; Tomsic 2017) but should be briefly recapped. Armstrong was born in 1950 in suburban Melbourne, the daughter of an amateur photographer father who sold real estate for a living, and primary school teacher mother. Without knowing exactly what she wanted to do and lacking Australian industry role models, Armstrong enrolled at the age of seventeen in the Swinburne School of Film and Television with the intention of studying production design. At Swinburne, she gained a passion for film but little in terms of formal training (i.e. how to work with actors, write a budget, or apply for grants). When she finished at Swinburne she sought what work was available in the fledgling and male-dominated industry, finding some work as an assistant editor. When she tried to gain employment at the ABC, she was told she would have to sit a typing test and to apply to the secretarial pool. Undaunted, Armstrong applied and was accepted into the then new national Australian Film and Television School (AFTS, now Australian Film, Television and Radio School, or AFTRS), which was a government initiative and cornerstone of the Australian film revival. AFTS was underwritten by a grant of $100,000 which was designed to jump-start the nation's industry (Chapman 2003). Film production in this period was tasked with creating distinctly Australian content and Armstrong was one of only two women in the school's first cohort of twelve. At AFTS she gained technical skills and professional connections that would sustain her through her career and ambition to make her mark in the newly revived industry.

Armstrong's enrolment in the very first cohort of the national film school and high-profile association with the 1970s Revival lend her a significance and recognisability on par with other globally recognised Australian directors, like Fred Schepisi, Peter Weir, and Bruce Beresford. Internationally, Armstrong's movies have been nominated and/or won prizes at pre-eminent festivals including Cannes (1979), Berlin (1985, 1992), London Critics Circle (1981), Chicago International (1981, 1982, and 2015), and Sundance (2006) and two high-profile American awards showcasing the accomplishments of women in the industry: Elle Women in Hollywood (1998) and Women in Film Crystal, Dorothy Arzner Director's award (1995). Domestically, Armstrong's career has been consistently recognised across four decades by the peak industry bodies, which include the Australian Directors Guild (2007, 2010) and the Australian Film Institute (1979, 1987, 1992, 1996, 2006). The ongoing relevance of Armstrong's authorship to Australian film history and cultural heritage is evidenced by the choice to include *My Brilliant Career* and *Starstruck* in the prestigious curated NFSA (National Film and Sound Archive) Restores programme.

Because of how her career stretches across many decades of seismic change in Australian and international filmmaking landscapes, including shifts in funding, marketing, distribution, and exhibition, and changes to a director's means of engagement with audiences through new social media technologies, Armstrong is also one of Australia's most experienced film directors. Her forty years in the industry have equipped her with the skills and adaptability to embody multiple discursive constructions of authorship and to deploy an authorial brand across industrial and civic contexts which surpass those of colleagues with fewer working years. Some of Armstrong's achievements as an author have been well accounted for. Her fiercely personal connections to her projects and the consistency of themes and concerns across multiple genres, including contemporary-set dramas, period dramas, the musical, and documentary, indicate an authorship in line with the auteur theory; the single book-length monograph dedicated to the director, Felicity Collins's *The Cinema of Gillian Armstrong*, confirms Armstrong to be an auteur in this sense.

What has received less examination to date are the contexts through which Armstrong became visible as an author early on, her own interpretation of factors underpinning her success, the meaning of her authorship in different contexts, and how her authorship has changed over time. Armstrong has from the very start of her career been quite visible to audiences and industry alike, but the means for this have shifted over the years, as have the parameters around her own authorial agency and its valuing in domestic vs in international contexts. Armstrong's authorship furthermore comprises significant contemporary iterations across social media and activist spaces, where she is able to make canny use of her name recognition to support and bring attention to new political causes, such as the 'Make It Australian' campaign.[2]

This chapter tracks the shifting and sometimes contradictory ways Armstrong has achieved visibility as an author over the course of her career and identifies the discursive dimensions within which her career as an Australian woman filmmaker became possible. It investigates the storying of Armstrong's success to determine the practical negotiations and working contexts that enabled her to succeed in frequently highly competitive environments. It argues that Armstrong's authorship is multivalent and changeable, with different meanings in different contexts. The chapter explores key themes in her authorship to date, as picked up by journalists and film critics and as espoused and forwarded by Armstrong herself, in particular within an oral history with Armstrong that was created in 2011 (Shirley 2011). Presenting these components both highlights the contexts and conditions under which Armstrong worked and continues to work and paints a broader picture of the diverse survival strategies available to women over the course of this long and complex period.

A multidimensional career

It is useful from the contemporary vantage point to recap the impressive multidimensionality of Armstrong's career, including her activity across such a diversity of generic and international cinema spaces. Trained at the start in both drama and documentary, Armstrong has remained fluid in her work experience in each. To summarise this fluidity: in 1976 Armstrong made the first of her five-part government-funded documentary series about three working-class teenage girls in South Australia (*Smokes and Lollies*). She followed this two years later with her break-out Australian drama, *My Brilliant Career* (1979),[3] which was in turn followed by the second in the five-part documentary series (*Fourteen's Good, Eighteen's Better* (1981)). After the success of *My Brilliant Career*, Armstrong avoided invitations for projects on (in Armstrong's words) 'women achievers' set in the past and opted instead to direct the quirky low-budget Australian musical comedy *Starstruck* (1982). After *Starstruck*, Armstrong landed a contract with MGM to direct the studio feature, *Mrs. Soffel* (1985). A return to Australia then enabled her to direct another small-budget drama (*High Tide* (1987)), followed by another iteration in her five-part documentary series (*Bingo, Bridesmaids & Braces* (1988)), followed by the small-budget Australian drama *The Last Days of Chez Nous* (1992). The commercially successful Columbia feature *Little Women* (1994) came next, followed by more documentaries (in 1996, 2006, 2010, and 2015) and further dramas, both Australian (*Oscar and Lucinda* (1997)), and international co-productions (*Charlotte Gray* (2001) and *Death Defying Acts* (2007)).

What ought to be immediately apparent from this sketch is Armstrong's professional agility making movies in many different contexts and national settings; for these aspects, Armstrong's career has been termed 'unorthodox' (Mordue 1989: 272) and 'unusual' (Caputo 1992: 6), yet it has also been said that the 'sideways steps have always led on to the next opportunity with a surprisingly logical, and fortuitous, grace' (Mordue 1989: 271). Armstrong's own analyses of the trajectory she has taken aligns with critical assessments such as these. She has spoken early on and repeatedly about the importance of not being pigeonholed as a director of either documentaries *or* dramas, period films *or* contemporary-set movies, transnational co-productions *or* local iterations and spoken positively about the heterogeneity of her directing opportunities. As Mordue writes: 'How many directors leave a Hollywood which still wants them [after directing *Mrs. Soffel*], return home to make a low-budget movie [*High Tide*], then follow it with a documentary on working-class women [*Bingo, Bridesmaids and Braces*]? Not many' (Mordue 1989: 272).

There is value in looking at Armstrong's relationship to documentary and its role in her career as a specific case-study illustration of the above, as documentary is often cast as a stepping stone to more commercially lucrative features in characterising a career trajectory. The common assumption is that a director opts for smaller-budget documentary at the start of their career, but once they land work in drama, they do not move back. This conventional understanding fails to capture the significance of documentary within Armstrong's oeuvre and her own self-positioning as a maker of both; it also potentially eclipses the recent attention documentary has received, as an expressive space especially for women directors (Ulfsdotter and Rogers 2018). While Armstrong sees herself primarily as a filmmaker of dramatic movies, she has spoken passionately about the documentaries she has made: '[T]his documentary is my baby. My personal story, I suppose' (Baker 1996). Comparing documentary with drama, she has said 'often in drama you start getting cut off from what's really going on in life' and 'documentaries are a great way to get out and find out how other people are living'. She has spoken positively about working on *Not Fourteen Again*, the fourth iteration of her long-format documentary series that she made after *Little Women*, claiming working with a small crew was 'sobering relief' from Hollywood filmmaking. '"Going back to having a crew of three and no limos at the airport and having to carry the tripod and sharing pub sandwiches, it does remind you of where I started"' (Schembri 1996: 12). Reflecting on the value of documentary four years later, she clarified, 'I didn't write the script for this one and I couldn't have. That's the thing you learn in documentary, that life is so much richer and so much more unexpected than fiction' (Hooks 1998: 3).

In addition to demonstrating documentary's significance for Armstrong's career, commentary such as this indicates Armstrong's understanding, which transcends genre, of the value of adaptability as a means to professional ends; in other words, the idea that Armstrong does not take any directing opportunities for granted. Perhaps because of the different industrial areas in which she has effectively worked, Armstrong's success has been polysemic; the discursive construction of her authorship means different things in the documentary context, for example, than in the context of drama, and with regards to the Australian industry compared to international ones.

Within the context of the medium-size English-language industry where 'brain drain' is a pervasive narrative (that is, domestically trained directors departing to find employment overseas, typically the United States), a recognised director like Armstrong who has succeeded in overseas environments but who then *rejects* subsequent overseas offers and chooses to return 'home' to work in Australia, is cause for local celebration.[4] Armstrong's first American feature *Mrs. Soffel* provided opportunities for Australian industry and fans to celebrate her success and her achievements as a young woman director were sometimes mapped on to a nationalist agenda. On occasion, American producers were constructed in the Australian press as the behemoth against which the brave director stood firm in the defence of a weaker but ultimately worthy national endeavour.

> The feminist spirits soar along with the nationalistic stirrings as one conjures up images of a plucky young female director at the helm of a production that few American women would get a crack at. Finally, there are the much publicized stories of this headstrong filmmaker steadfastly holding off armies of studio executives who want to dilute her vision … and winning! Now we're really cooking: a female David taking on a polyester-clad Goliath … an artist locking horns with businessmen … a proud Aussie battler returning to her native shores in triumph … a woman assaulting a male bastion. The right ingredients are there. (Enker 1985: 27)

The small scale of Armstrong's movies – including her choice not to neglect documentaries – has especially promoted domestic celebration, perhaps on account of their marked contrast with the big budget opportunities seemingly on offer in Hollywood. For example, Rosemary Neill has pointed out that she turned down 'lucrative overseas offers' to make *Bingo, Bridesmaids* (1988: 141). In interviews with the Australian press, Armstrong perpetuates such a pro-Australian approach. On numerous occasions she has spoken glowingly about, and proclaimed she has benefited from, her experiences in the Australian industry, including her training, testifying for example that after working in Hollywood on *Little Women*, she found working in Australia a salve and a delight (Robson 1997). She has on such occasions spoken harshly of the American studio production context and noted how lucky Australians have been.

In international spheres, Armstrong's authorship has been celebrated for reasons that are subtly different. Lisa French has assessed the role played by women in international perceptions of Australian cinema and the Australian film industry as a whole. She notes that women are proportionately more numerous at awards ceremonies than their colleagues who are men, both domestically and internationally, and that the Australian industry is characterised as broadly supportive of women practitioners to make a global contribution (2014: 663). These assessments of the positive regard of the international community extend to Armstrong: Americans in particular noted her plucky determination and mapped it neatly on to images they held of Australians as hard-working battlers. In discussions about Armstrong's career, American critics celebrated Australian women directors as less expensive than US directors and in possession of the 'bite and vision' to make something other than 'soft-centered "women's movies"' (Taylor 1995: 78). Other aspects that attracted them were what they perceived to be a lack of commercialism: 'Americans don't appear to enjoy the ambiguity of women with complicated motives, or the threat of female hostility, unless it's gussied up with guns to mimic male aggression or blacklace teddies to cater to male fantasy' (Taylor 1995: 80). Armstrong's heroines,

Judy Davis in particular, received praise for being 'triumphantly awkward' (Wood 1998: 44), in contrast to Armstrong herself, who 'couldn't be more accommodating' (Wood 1998: 44). As mentioned earlier in this chapter, Armstrong's value has been recognised via two significant awards targeting women's accomplishments, the Elle Women in Hollywood Awards (Icon award 1998) and Women in Film Crystal Awards (Dorothy Arzner Directors Award 1995).

Perceptions of success: Armstrong's point of view

When Armstrong is called upon to name the factors which contributed to her success, she is characteristically modest, frequently citing ineffable factors such as 'dumb luck'. When pressed, she credits the training she received in the Australian film school, the supportive professional environment, and the government funding for production and (in her case) travel which followed. There are two further and interrelated factors she credits for playing a role in her own success as a filmmaker; these are the relationship with producers and studio, and the relationship with crew and casting.

Australian screen sector researcher Anthony Johnson describes the role of a film producer as someone who is engaged from the development of an idea through to post-production and distribution of a film (2014). Aspects of the producer's job will include identifying and securing financing for the project, signing personnel (including actors, scriptwriters, directors, and people in below-the-line positions), managing budgets (including schedule blow-outs), and delivering product in line with what investors were promised. Producers typically are involved in distribution, which in the US may require test screenings which in turn provide op-portunities for producers to adjust publicity and release strategies and which may affect levels of support.

A common theme threading through all nearly all of Armstrong's positive involvements is the relationship she has been able to establish with producers and the respective producing studio; in most cases, producers have exerted power to approve and make changes to budgets, shoot schedules and locations, casting choices and terms, attached production personnel, and even language of the production. A positive relationship with a supportive producer in Armstrong's opinion, tends to yield a good outcome for most of these aspects; conversely, working with producers Armstrong has deemed weak has typically meant a less than optimal outcome.

In describing the context surrounding women and Australian screen production in the 1980s, Mary Tomsic identifies a cohort of women producers who became visible across the Australian film landscape at this time; these included Joan Long, Margaret Fink, Pat Lovell, Jan Chapman, Sandra Levy, and others (2017). There is no doubt that Armstrong's domestic productions have benefited from positive and supportive relations with producers Fink (*My Brilliant Career*), Chapman (*The Last Days of Chez Nous*), Sandra Levy (*High Tide*), and Robin Dalton (*Oscar and Lucinda*); the success of her international productions has likewise tended to rise and fall on the strength and commitment and relations with the producer. Armstrong's best overseas experiences have come about largely because of the loyalty, experience, and commitment of the team of producers attached to the project: for example Armstrong has spoken highly of Denise Di Novi's commitment to the project of *Little Women* and of that of Edgar Scherick and Scott Rudin to *Mrs. Soffel*.[5]

Casting and crew

In Armstrong's opinion, the second factor which exerts a strong influence on the outcome of a production is the production crew and the cast. Filmmaking is a collaborative effort whose success rises and falls depending on the strength of the team as a whole, and Armstrong is well aware of this. With some variation across the body of her work, Armstrong has negotiated in international spheres to maintain contractual arrangements with people known to her throughout her career; a scrutiny of production credits of her international productions reveals a recurrence of Australian industry professionals. These include Nicholas Beauman (editor on *Mrs. Soffel, Little Women, Charlotte Gray,* and *Death Defying Acts,* as well as on Armstrong's domestically produced movies *The Singer and the Dancer, My Brilliant Career, Starstruck, High Tide, Bingo, Bridesmaids & Braces, The Last Days of Chez Nous, Oscar and Lucinda, Unfolding Florence, Love, Lust & Lies,* and *Women He's Undressed*); Russell Boyd (cinematographer for *Mrs. Soffel* and the Australian productions *The Singer and the Dancer, Starstruck,* and *High Tide*); Geoffrey Simpson (cinematographer for *Little Women, The Last Days of Chez Nous,* and *Oscar and Lucinda*); Mark Turnbull (assistant director on *Starstruck, High Tide, The Last Days of Chez Nous, Little Women, Oscar and Lucinda, Charlotte Gray,* and *My Brilliant Career* [where he was second AD]); Dion Beebe (cinematographer, *Charlotte Gray*); and Luciana Arrighi (production design for *Mrs. Soffel* and for the Australian productions *My Brilliant Career, Oscar and Lucinda,* and *Starstruck* [for which she did costume design]).[6]

Casting for nearly all of Armstrong's overseas productions has tended to comprise a multinational mix of emerging and established stars: Diane Keaton, Mel Gibson, and Matthew Modine in *Mrs. Soffel*; Winona Ryder, Kirsten Dunst, Susan Sarandon in *Little Women*; Greta Scacchi and Jimmy Smits in *Fires Within*; Cate Blanchett and Billy Crudup in *Charlotte Gray*; Guy Pearce, Catherine Zeta-Jones, and Saoirse Ronan in *Death Defying Acts*. Though Armstrong has not been decisive in all of these hiring decisions (for example Ryder was already signed on to *Little Women,* before Armstrong came onboard), there is evidence that Armstrong acted as a draw for actors in other instances to join a project, and/or played a substantive role in actors' positive experiences. Some actors have opted to work with her repeatedly (Blanchett, Alvarado, Davis), and Armstrong is known for her mentoring of less-experienced actors, such as Jo Kennedy and Ross O'Donovan in *Starstruck,* Kirsten Dunst in *Little Women,* and Claudia Karvan in *High Tide.* Armstrong's skill with new actors such as Davis, Karvan, Blanchett, and Gibson has been noted: 'No director working in the world today has so consistently drawn so many great performances and roles for leading women actors, or managed the complex net of relationships from teenage girls to adult women and aging matriarchs with such eloquence' (Mordue 1992: 64).

Taken together, Armstrong's activities in the areas of casting and crew composition are not insignificant but give evidence of both Armstrong's clout overseas and her imbrication across the space of the Australian filmmaking industry. They indicate the unique way she responds to the pressures of transnationalism while maintaining a localised value. As Ryan and Goldsmith claim, transnationalism does not mean the simple erasure of earlier iterations but often their incorporation of them: 'the national continues to exert the force of its presence even within transnational film-making practices' (2017: 6, quoting Will Higbee and Song Hwee Lim).

In the introduction to their special edition of the journal *Camera Obscura* 'The Place of the Contemporary Female Director', Therese Davis and Belinda Smaill use the phrase 'between worlds' to shed light on the current industrial and cultural landscape in which female directors work and through which they are framed (2014: 1). Like the directors included in the special edition, Armstrong's authorship is characterised by dexterity, multi-sited industrial competence, and success that has not stayed static over the years.

Images of Armstrong

Numerous studies of women's film authorship note the journalistic focus on the matter of physical appearance, sometimes in lieu of a director's career accomplishments. While Dorothy Arzner, for example, was pictured in ways that challenged established codes of femininity, Kathryn Bigelow obtained visibility as a maverick (Mayne 1994; Tasker 2010). In the cases of both directors, recurring images have been reified to become tropes that both constrain and enable the visibility of the respective director.

Like Arzner and Bigelow, Armstrong has been cast in terms that focus disproportionately on her image, mostly in terms that line up with established codes of heterosexual femininity. In the first ten years of her career especially, journalists and interviewers often remarked on her physical attractiveness, her 'pleasant' look, and the 'softness' of her voice and demeanour, leaning on comments or images that emphasised heterosexual femininity and glamour.

For example in this illustration from producer and journalist Sue Mathews's *Conversations with Five Directors* (1984), Armstrong is shown in a glamourous, alluring head shot, without camera or gear, and staring straight out at the photographer (Figure 1.1) (Mathews 1984: 116). Unremarkable on its own, the distinctiveness of this image becomes apparent when compared with images of colleagues Peter Weir (Mathews 1984: 68) and John Duigan (Figure 1.2) (Mathews 1984: 174) from the same book, or with photos of Australian directors Simon Wincer (Figure 1.3) (White 1984: 110) and George Miller, from a different book but taken the very same year (Figure 1.4) (White 1984: 92).

Figure 1.1 Gillian Armstrong, from Sue Mathews (1984), *35mm Dreams: Conversations with Five Directors* (p. 116). Photographer: Stuart Campbell. Estate of Stuart Campbell

Figure 1.2 John Duigan, from Sue Mathews (1984), *35mm Dreams: Conversations with Five Directors* (p. 174). Photographer: Carolyn Johns

A vocabulary through which to explain these differing sets of images can be enlisted from a key article published in 1982, just three years after Armstrong's first feature. Richard Dyer's now canonical essay 'Don't Look Now: The Male Pin-up' compares and contrasts images of male and female models with respect to what Dyer believed to be a relay of looks (Dyer 1982). Dyer noted the challenges posed by male pin-ups to the relay of looks that he identified. He termed this an instability, to indicate male pin-ups' apparent failure to participate in the exchange of looks that typifies female models' engagement, that is, to cooperate within the gendered economies of visual entertainment. Rather than staring straight out into the camera in what ought to be a complicit way, the male model's stance or eyeline works to thwart such an engagement. They either appear to direct their

Figure 1.3 Simon Wincer, from David White (1984), *Australian Movies to the World: The International Success of Australian Films since 1970* (p. 110). Entertainment Media Pty Ltd

eyes towards something off-screen, not in the direction of the camera. Or, their physical stance suggests their engagement with modelling is accidental and that they just happen to have been caught in the middle of a different activity, while the photo was snapped. In Dyer's examples, they're wearing gear that suggests a more appropriate physical activity than modelling – sports or construction gear, for example. Female models, in contrast, are willing and complicit in the modelling task, signalling agreement by staring straight into the camera and appearing to meet the audience's gaze, and associated either with no props or props that are inexpertly handled.

It isn't difficult to apply Dyer's ideas to the marketing strategies and journalist commentary about Armstrong from this early phase of her career. The obvious conclusion to draw from these images is that journalists struggled with knowing how to value or make sense of Armstrong's contribution at this time; let's remember

Figure 1.4 George Miller, from David White (1984), *Australian Movies to the World: The International Success of Australian Films since 1970* (p. 100). Entertainment Media Pty Ltd

she was famously the first Australian woman to direct a movie in Australia since the McDonagh sisters in the 1930s. To co-opt phrasing from another well-known film theorist from this period, Armstrong was herself often made the object of the look, rather than its agent, objectified, rather than the source of the images herself (Mulvey 1990/1975).

A survey of a second set of images and tropes would seem to underscore this. In these images and popular descriptions, Armstrong's significance is conflated with those of her leading

Figure 1.5 Gillian Armstrong, from David White (1984), *Australian Movies to the World: The International Success of Australian Films since 1970* (p. 66). Entertainment Media Pty Ltd

Figure 1.6 Diane Keaton and Mel Gibson, from *Mrs. Soffel*, Edgar Scherick Associates and MGM, 1984. Dir. Gillian Armstrong

female actors and/or characters in her movies or documentaries; the labour that Armstrong performs behind the camera is understood via the labour that is performed in front of it. For example, in one photo, Armstrong's appearance resembles that of Dianne Keaton in *Mrs. Soffel* (Figure 1.5) (White 1984: 66); Armstrong is pictured in a fur hat, resembling this image of Diane Keaton, in a fur coat, from *Mrs. Soffel* (1984) (Figure 1.6).

Mark Mordue conjures an image of Armstrong's teenage self, to strike an allegiance between her and the girls at the centre of her documentary series, *The Story of Kerry, Josie and Diana*: 'like most teenagers she wished she was thinner and had long straight hair. She felt less than perfect, less than desirable . . .' (Mordue 1989: 270). In *The Australian Women's Weekly*, Christine Hogan links Armstrong to the lead character Sybylla in *My Brilliant Career*: 'when she was making "My Brilliant Career", her first feature film and Miles Franklin's autobiography, she could have been a 1970s manifestation of Sybylla' (Hogan 1982: 62). Hogan then noted how Armstrong's 'look' changed from movie to movie: 'the neat and restrained young woman who made "My Brilliant Career" has given way to the up-to-date starlet promoting her latest film, "Starstruck"' (1982: 62).

Research on the history of women in the silent screen along with other work has shifted and called for more expansive ideas of what it means to be a director, with data showing the breadth of roles typically occupied by women in the screen industries in the silent era, which often included acting and directing, as well as producing and other elements. I don't want to dismiss the labour of either the researchers who helpfully bring this information to light or the value of the women's contributions in the silent era. But I do want to distinguish them from Australia in 1974, which, just prior to the introduction of colour television, was a 68-million-dollar-per-year industry, and no longer allowed the career porousness described by Stamp (2015) and others. The recourse to interpret Armstrong through the frame of one or more actresses, or subjects in one of her documentaries, misreads and seems to minimise the power and control that Armstrong actually enjoyed as a key figure both in the domestic industry and, with *Little Women* (1994), one of the few women at the time to helm an American studio film grossing more than $50 million.[7]

Or does it? The tendency to interpret this focus on women's appearance as something disempowering and incompatible with ideas of authority and expertise, is itself a theoretical hold-over from ideas of feminist film theory in the mid/late 1970s from Laura Mulvey, John Berger, and others which interpreted entertainment's address to spectators along strictly gendered lines without any allowance for female agency. Since they first appeared, these ideas have of course been challenged and contoured by critical race studies and queer theorists among others and recast in light of cyclical opportunities for women's agency in forms like 1980s horror's 'the final girl' and post-*Bridesmaids* 'womance' comedies (see Clover 1992; Whitley 2018).

Let me return to some of the journalistic commentary mentioned above. After noting Armstrong's wanting to be thin and to have long straight hair as alluded to above, Mark Mordue continues: 'some 21 years later, this almost laughably typical act of adolescent self-consciousness nevertheless helps Armstrong to begin explaining her empathy with the three once-upon-a-time teenage girls whose paths to adulthood she has sporadically recorded' (1989). Christie Hogan, in *Women's Weekly*, concludes the comment (also mentioned above) with a caution that 'the public should beware the day she [Armstrong] decides to make a horror film' (1982: 62), such is her passion for 'taking on the persona appropriate to her films [to market them]' (1982: 62).

From these two writers, it appears there may be greater agency and benefit in the historical focus on Armstrong's appearance than may initially be evident, in other words, that these statements attribute a greater degree of control than first appears. While the emphasis on Armstrong's appearance would seem at first glance to position her as a disempowered professional, that is, an object or victim of the press which is unused to representing women in positions of creative control, a closer look reveals a person well in charge of her own self-presentation and a strategic deployment of such tropes. Using the means available to her and in the terms of the day, Armstrong takes a subtle but active role in her own self-construction to rewrite dominant journalistic narratives.

These issues – the disproportionate focus on looks and appearance, and Armstrong's ability to package artistic control under the more acceptable theme of feminine modesty – become all the more apparent in the middle phase of Armstrong's career. Journalistic interest in her looks and image do not go away, but Armstrong parries questions on such topics for her own purposes. Thirteen years after the above-mentioned article by Christine Hogan and on the eve of her blockbuster success with *Little Women*, Armstrong participates in an interview with a reporter from *The New York Times* in 1995, who poses the question of Armstrong's age. The reporter comments:

> Gillian Armstrong does not immediately answer. She pushes her smooth blond hair away from her face with blunt, sensible fingers and smiles. She takes her time. 'Just say early 40's,' she finally replies. She is not being coy. She is politely serving notice that this interview will be conducted on her terms; the woman who became Australia's first female film director at age 27 is accustomed to being in charge. (Reichl 1995: B1)

As these comments hopefully begin to suggest, Armstrong's own self-positioning on issues of appearance and personal style with which they are often connected both deflect journalistic fascinations of the time and serve as the basis from which Armstrong is able to launch a subtle but staunch critique of industry sexism from what we would now term a feminist point of view. While Armstrong appears to have been cast as what Mulvey would term an object of the look, and – as I will go on to show – maintained an ambivalence to being classed as 'feminist' at this time in her career, her own response to matters of appearance and 'feminine style' are far less straightforward than they first appear.

On the issue of the link between professional directorial competence and appearance, Armstrong has had plenty to say. In interviews she has attacked the narrow conceptualising of women directors and mocked prevalent media misconstructions. She has lashed out at the media's masculinist conception of directing. Ironic humour is a potent weapon in her toolkit. She has said: 'When I meet people they look surprised and say "Oh, *you're* the woman director. You don't look anything like I expected you to look"' (Mathews 1984: 162). She recalls 'When the Australian press came down to the set of *My Brilliant Career*, all writing stories about this freak woman director. A lot of them still had that idea of . . . somebody with jodhpurs and a megaphone, and they were so disappointed' (Mathews 1984: 157).[8]

Armstrong has noted the trope of journalists wanting to depict directors through their female stars, as another failure of insight. In an interview with *Washington Post* reporter Megan Rosenfeld (1983), Armstrong quipped that after *My Brilliant Career* people assumed she would be conservative and contained and would expect '[she] wore [her] hair in a bun and stayed home embroidering and listening to Schumann'.

While the accounts which I have just described indicate a journalistic underestimation of Armstrong's directorial authority, interestingly in her own understanding and those of a handful of sympathetic insiders, these very same style concerns are repositioned as assets. For example, Sue Mathews comments

'From her student films on, visual flair and a strong concern for the appearance of things have characterised all of Armstrong's films. An interest in style is evident even in the way Gillian Armstrong looks herself: her dress is studied, yet casual and idiosyncratic' (Mathews 1984: 118). According to Armstrong, this personal 'visual flair' coupled with her knowledge of period style helped make her 1930s-set short period film *One Hundred a Day* authentic. Armstrong comments: 'Well, half the costumes were my dresses! . . . And because of the designer training in me I wanted to have all those things absolutely right. . . . I wanted everything to be absolutely authentic' (Mathews 1984: 132). In another account, she claims the writer of *Starstruck* granted her permission to direct his script, based on an unusual and striking pair of shoes Armstrong was seen wearing. In these testimonies and elsewhere, Armstrong's own 'idiosyncratic' style sense is positioned to have a positive influence on her professional success.

Through testimony such as this, it seems Armstrong has been able to fashion her long-lasting interest in style into a means to assist in production and pre-production processes. In interviews, she has been able to merge this interest in style with a psychological insight into the pressures placed on girls in particular to conform to specific and narrow standards of beauty, to make progressive casting choices. For example, in the casting of *Little Women*, Armstrong has described how Wynona Ryder was initially thought to be too glamourous for the tomboy character Jo. Armstrong defended the casting through an appeal to historical notions of beauty and argued that (in Victorian times) Ryder would have actually not been considered a conventional beauty at all: 'The way women are so often portrayed throughout the history of cinema is by putting them into very simple boxes, often by men. So to equate a woman who wants a career as being a plain tomboy is a terrible cliché. It's dreadful to think that just because Jo is a tomboy she doesn't care about how she looks, and because she is a woman not interested in the conventional mores of society does not necessarily mean she has to be ugly' (Armstrong 1999: 106). Further demonstration of this insight is evident in her choice to accept the invitation to direct *My Brilliant Career*. Armstrong describes how she took on the project based on comments she said she heard about the movie's principal character: 'There was a comment made to me by someone early on, "oh, so you're going to have to cast someone that is really plain, as the girl?", and . . . it was a man that said that to me, and I thought that a man cannot make this film, because they don't understand that every adolescent girl thinks they're plain' (Thompson 1983).

In spite of the ten-year difference separating these two anecdotes, they demonstrate Armstrong's nuanced and contextualised understanding of women's and girls' feelings about beauty, and deployment of these insights for professional ends; her willingness to advocate for an approach that may initially appear iconoclastic; her support for individuated casting methods and commitment to assessing women's contributions in ways not based on stereotypes; and her unusual take on familiar themes of professional and personal discreditation based on women's failure to live up to conventional expectations of appearance. Armstrong's resistance to belittling and objectifying narratives about 'feminine' appearance and her ownership of themes of style on her terms is one powerful means which allowed her to create a different and important space for herself within masculinist spheres of film production. This push-back via seemingly trivial discussions about appearance and so forth are also the principal means Armstrong had at her disposal to voice stances which we would now term feminist.

Armstrong, feminism, and on being a 'woman director'

The impact of Armstrong's gender has been a subject of journalistic fascination since the beginning, with the result that she often expressed frustration with critics who cared more about her gender than the work she was producing, and sometimes appeared to be dodging questions about the feminist content of her movies or her own feminist politics. Since those early days, Armstrong has risen to become Australia's highest profile advocate for women in media production. She currently serves as advisor to Gender Matters, the national suite of initiatives designed to address gender imbalance within the national screen industry, and frequently speaks out against the challenges that women in the industry face and of ongoing need for support.

From the moment she first entered the public arena, Armstrong's gender attracted journalistic interest. When Armstrong, Judy Davis, and producer Margaret Fink travelled to Cannes for the screening of *My Brilliant Career* in 1979, the press approached them with bemused curiosity, noting the incongruity of the idea of a woman director, and repeatedly highlighting the team's gender (Cannes news footage 1979). Writing in *Cleo*, Sue Ellen O'Grady quipped '[I]t's hard to believe that anyone who looks so young and so completely lacks any air of authority could be a film director, the vocation for full-blown egos and giant vocal cords'; O'Grady continued, 'some thought the idea of women making a film just too cute for words' (O'Grady 1979: 65).

In the 1970s when Armstrong got her start, the cultural and industrial climate was an uneven mix of entrenched sexism, new opportunities, and feminist activisms. In interviews Armstrong has recalled the poor treatment of women workers, low expectations placed on women who wanted to enter the industry, and extra challenges women faced when they began to work. She has also recalled the pressure she experienced to join activist groups and to tell certain kinds of stories, which, according to her, she largely resisted. Although Armstrong claimed sympathy with the political ambitions of feminist filmmaking organisations like the Sydney Women's Film Group (formed in 1971) and the Women's Film Fund (formed in 1975), she claimed a lack of fit between their political aspirations and her commercial ambitions and never felt drawn to join them. In interviews, Armstrong has long and consistently expressed perceptions of such a lack of fit. In 1979 she stated 'Although I am very involved in the women's movement, it hasn't ever liked me much. My films aren't strong enough' (Williamson 1979: 19). In 1984 she claimed her movies were sometimes judged negatively because of their commercial ambitions: audiences 'didn't like the ending' of *The Singer and the Dancer* (Mathews 1984: 137). And as recently as 2017 she again reiterated that some political filmmaking groups had 'looked down on' her films (Hall 2017).

Armstrong's expressed ambivalence towards some 1970s feminist filmmaking groups and dissociation from their political aims have however not succeeded in shielding her own work from sexist reviews, namely from the perception that it includes feminist themes. Writing in the *Washington Post* about *Mrs. Soffel*, Paul Attanasio suggested that the inclusion of feminist elements made her movies irrelevant:

> Armstrong seems to have embarked on a sort of filmic PhD in women's studies, dredging up historical examples of femmes fatales who transcended times in which their career and sexual aspirations were denied. But these battles were fought, and won, years ago. Victorianism was bad for women – who cares? (Attanasio 1985)

In Attanasio's formulation, Armstrong's interest in telling stories featuring women characters was deemed unworthy and held against her. Even in positive reviews, a film's excellence was at times deemed to depend upon its suppression of feminist themes:

> Armstrong's best work ('My Brilliant Career,' 'High Tide,' 'The Last Days of Chez Nous') has featured young, independent women who go against the traditional social grain to fulfill their creative and personal dreams. *Yet to describe her as a feminist filmmaker is to limit her achievements within ideological constraints*, for her remarkable talent is largely based on her clear-eyed observation of human relationships in all their magnetism, folly and untidiness. (Levy 1997) (emphasis added)

In these formulations, feminism is aligned with an ideology that is dull and constrained, an aesthetically limiting liability that filmmakers take on at their peril.

Throughout her career, Armstrong has often been asked about the importance of gender to her success, her feelings about the phrase 'woman director', and her relationship to feminism. In the early days Armstrong found many of these questions to be a burden and resented being constantly asked to speak on the issues. She pointed out the unfair double standard which required women to spend time commenting on their gender: 'Who goes to Philip Noyce's films and writes about how his films show an interest in men?' (McFarlane 2008: 20).[9] But in spite of the distance Armstrong may have felt from feminist groups at the time, her dismissal of feminism in the early days was never straightforward and her answers often expressed an ambivalence that frustrated researchers seeking a more clear-cut endorsement of feminist principles. For example, a 1979 interviewer in *Cleo* plainly reports that she is not a feminist but then includes a quotation from Armstrong which states, 'Well, I suppose I am a feminist, but not in a heavy way' (O'Grady 1979: 66). A response Armstrong gives, ten years later, to an interviewer in *Sight and Sound* both indicates her desire to opt out of the 'woman filmmaker' category and attempts to preserve the possibility that women filmmakers do offer a unique perspective: 'I consider myself an individual, and so you should compare my work to that of any other filmmaker, male or female, because every artist should be different ... But then again, there *are* things that are different about female perceptions' (Mordue 1989: 271).

Even as Armstrong declined to attach herself to political causes, she expressed an interest in women's experiences; and from the very beginning of her career, Armstrong asserted the value in making movies about subjects that speak to a director's experience. Most of the short films Armstrong made in the years before she made her first dramatic feature tell stories of specifically gendered experiences, such as the stifling and repetitive nature of women's work inside the home and the challenge of obtaining an abortion. As described in this book's introduction, *The Roof Needs Mowing* captured both the intense claustrophobia experienced by middle-class housewives and the feelings of stasis felt by breadwinner husbands. Armstrong's award-winning, 1930s-set *One Hundred A Day*, about a woman seeking an abortion, put Armstrong on the map of the fledgling Australian industry and signalled her interest in themes of gender inequity and disadvantage. When Armstrong succeeded to feature films, she continued to be drawn to stories of specifically gendered challenges, with the majority continuing to centre on women's experiences. Armstrong's first feature, *My Brilliant Career*, confirmed her interest in telling stories from a woman's point of view, as did subsequent projects. Social justice concerns such as women's financial independence and not wanting to be defined by a male partner are embraced and promulgated by many of Armstrong's movie characters, including the girls in her five-part longitudinal documentary series.[10]

Present-day activisms: *Gender Matters* and *Make It Australian*

In the twenty-first century and in the face of entrenched and dismal statistics about women's low participation in media industries, Armstrong has refashioned herself as a vocal, emphatic, unequivocal, and energetic political crusader for women's increased participation in the Australian film industry. She has spoken frequently and passionately about the appalling statistics surrounding women's participation as directors in film industries around the world and attached herself to programmes for change (Hall 2017), the most visible of which is the national Gender Matters initiative, a suite of activities designed to address gender imbalance within the Australian screen industry. She has decried the differences in attitudes young males wanting to enter the industry encounter vs the attitudes young women contend with, and the process by which the 'young guy who did the jokey film . . . the funny fart-joke film – he gets invited to meet the advertising people' (Raj 2015: 11).

Armstrong has reflected on the personal change she herself has had to undergo to transform from someone who resisted recognising the need for women's initiatives, to someone who ardently now supports them; and in so doing, she may be opening space for others to adopt such a change of heart (Douglas 2016). She has acknowledged the fallacy of her 'young and snobby' thinking when (as a younger director) she thought that 'talent should be the only denominator of success' (Raj 2015: 10–11). In addition to her activism regarding women and the media, Armstrong has historically been active as an informal advocate for girls' education (Tripp 2010). For many years she has been a passionate supporter of Australian-produced media content and of government support for Australian media. Armstrong has spoken on and/or keynoted the subject at numerous occasions and most recently loaned her support to Make It Australian, the campaign to increase government funding and other mechanisms for Australian-produced media (Quinn 2017).

While Armstrong's feature-film-directing activities appear to be slowing, she has an engaged and observable public presence in social media spaces and uses her Twitter account to influence and generate awareness about all the above-named causes: women, women and media, Australian media, and Australian and global politics more generally. In the sixteen months after Armstrong first joined Twitter in 2017, she generated over 500 original tweets – a little more than one tweet per day, not including retweets. Most of these tweets evidence an effort to 'keep feminism on the public radar' (Taylor 2014: 761), build on prior activities, and send messages of endorsement, promotion, and encouragement, often to other women.

The ambiguities of celebrity feminism have a long history and have been outlined in relation to Germaine Greer and many others (see Taylor 2014; Negra and Holmes 2011; Projansky 2014; Savigny and Warner 2015; Turner 2004; Wicke 1994). While some have regretted the rise of the celebrity feminist, others recognise the power conferred by celebrity status and the important role celebrities may play in public culture to shape public discourse. Anthea Taylor cites Jennifer Wicke's claim that the celebrity field is more complex than previously recognised and that feminists would do well not to dismiss the labours of Germaine Greer and, I would argue, Gillian Armstrong as inauthentic. Lisa Tsaliki coins the term 'celebvocate' and examines how their public engagements – particularly on Twitter – may extend a person's impact on the public sphere and open new forms of engagement (Tsaliki 2016: 236). While Tsaliki found that some politicians and celebrity activists do not use Twitter effectively, my qualitative study of Armstrong's tweets between the time when she gained her Twitter account (in January 2017) and sixteen months later (to May 2018), showed that her Twitter is mostly populated with content relating to female filmmakers and general feminist sentiment and the second-largest group of tweets pertains to Australian films and filmmakers. Armstrong writes frequently about her own work and tweets about major events as they happen: for example, in October 2017 she tweeted almost exclusively about Harvey Weinstein and frequently about the 'Yes' vote for the Australian Poll for Same Sex Marriage. Armstrong's tweeting appears to capitalise on the social networks between her and her Twitter followers to effectively spread the word for political causes (Tsaliki 2016: 238).

Conclusion

Armstrong's authorship cannot be reduced to a unitary meaning. In this it is congruent with themes of women's contemporary film authorship more broadly. I have discussed Davis's and Smaill's phrase 'between worlds' earlier in this chapter and the applicability of this phrase for Armstrong. In their introduction to *Indie Reframed*, Linda Badley, Claire Perkins, and Michele Schreiber suggest that 'women filmmakers must work in between nationalities and genres through a variety of forms, vectors and roles whether to effect social change or simply to survive' (Badley et al. 2016: 13). Working for many decades across many continents and genres and industrial contexts, Gillian Armstrong has not been a passive actor but has performatively reached across and into multiple industrial contexts to craft her own methodologies and means of approach. She has adopted and refashioned discourses of female authorship in unique ways to maximise her positioning as a female director in times of both opportunity and uncertainty in the Australian film industry, as it has transformed from the publicly owned, national enterprise that it was in the 1970s to what Ben Goldsmith and others have termed an international cinema (Goldsmith 2010). Armstrong has proved to be a most adaptable public figure and has managed to operate and utilise her public persona for activist causes across socially and technologically quite diverse moments, both before and after social media. This chapter has demonstrated that Armstrong has embodied multiple versions of author over the years. She has not let herself be defined by prevailing and sometimes sexist discourses but has performatively crafted her own approach, remaking familiar components of female authorship in new ways to augment her positioning as a women director at a time of major transformation in the Australian film industry.

Notes

1 Book series include *Visionaries* (Edinburgh), journals include *Feminist Media Histories* (Berkeley), conferences include *Women and the Silent Screen* and *Doing Women's Film and Television Histories*, and networks include *Women Film History Network* (UK/Ireland).
2 *Make It Australian* lobbies the Australian government to support the industry and increase Australian content on television and online. Available at <https://makeitaustralian.com/> (last accessed 6 April 2020).
3 It may be worth noting that *My Brilliant Career* in 1979 was put into official competition at Cannes and later won six AFI awards including Best Film.
4 MGM offered her a three-picture contract after *Mrs. Soffel* but she chose to return to Australia instead (Mordue 1989: 272).
5 In contrast, of *Death Defying Acts* Armstrong claimed there was a 'cover up' about the budget which fell short; according to Armstrong, they had to find ways to cut, to the detriment of the film (Shirley 2011).
6 Armstrong specifically states on this and on 'all American contracts' she brought her choice of DOP (Geoffrey Simpson), own first assistant, and own editor (Nicholas Beauman) (Shirley 2011).

7   Surpassed by *Big* (1988, dir. Penny Marshall, lifetime gross 115M), *A League of Their Own* (1992, also dir. Marshall; lifetime gross 107M), *Sleepless in Seattle* (1993, dir. Nora Ephron, lifetime gross 126M), *The Prince of Tides* (1991, dir. Barbra Streisand, lifetime gross 74M).

8   'I think they selected me [to make *Smokes and Lollies*] because I've always looked a lot younger than I am and I could go out and mingle with fourteen year olds and not be noticed' (Mathews 1984: 147); 'Occasionally people have tripped over me and realised that I was the one who was whispering the commands to somebody' (Mathews 1984: 157).

9   For a longer comment from Armstrong on this subject, see her reflections: 'When I made my first feature film, being a woman was all anyone ever asked me about. It really, really annoyed me and I found it quite sexist in the end. I thought, "You know what – I'm just me and this is a Gillian Armstrong film". Not all women are going to do the same films and the same stories, and I was really put in this box, because it was a feminist story in a lot of ways, they thought that's all I ever wanted to talk about' (Hall 2017).

10 Armstrong has justified her interest in women's stories via her own knowledge: 'The stories that I read and the stories that I react to, so often have a female character. And it hasn't been, and for my part, a political decision that I want to make a story about a woman, it's because I can see the world through her eyes' (French 2018: 16). French is here citing her own interview with Armstrong.

2

A popular, commercial cinema: *Mrs. Soffel, Little Women, Charlotte Gray, Death Defying Acts*

From the very start of her career, Gillian Armstrong knew she wanted to make popular films with broad appeal, for the commercial movie industry. Shortly after her 1979 feature-film success, Armstrong found herself on the receiving end of numerous invitations to direct movies outside of Australia. Five years after *My Brilliant Career* screened at Cannes, Armstrong accepted an invitation to direct her first international feature, *Mrs. Soffel*, for MGM. Since that first feature, Armstrong has used her considerable clout to ensure the inclusion of Australian crew on all of her overseas productions; to date she is credited for five international commercial feature films: *Mrs. Soffel* (MGM, 1984), *Fires Within* (MGM, 1991), and *Little Women* (Columbia, 1994), made in the United States, and two European/UK co-productions, *Charlotte Gray* (Ecosse/Film Four/Warner Bros, 2001) and *Death Defying Acts* (Australian Film Finance Corporation/Myriad/BBC Films/Zephyr Films, 2007).

As a set of movies with recurring and recognisable characters, iconography, and settings, genre films are a product of an industrial model of production that relies on replicable production components and guaranteed audiences. Film genres provide an ideal balance of novelty and sameness and shape audience expectation into what Steve Neale has called regimes of expectation (Neale 2012: 179). As Mark David Ryan states, 'movie genres are universal story types which inform production, distribution and consumption' (2010: 844). I will return to the matter of the 'universal' in the next chapter when I discuss

Armstrong's Australian-set popular movies; in this chapter I am less concerned with national receptions than with Armstrong's 'incursions' into generic discourses (Zecchi 2018) and activation of what Harrod and Paszkiewicz term the 'generative force' of genre in the service of women's stories (2018: 10).

This chapter is the first of two chapters which examines, in a chronological order, Armstrong's achievements within the sometimes socially and aesthetically conservative space of popular genre movies. This chapter focuses on Armstrong's internationally produced movies: *Mrs. Soffel, Little Women, Charlotte Gray,* and *Death Defying Acts*. All of these films make use of period film conventions, hinge their stories around a complex and dynamic female protagonist, and offer a unique perspective on women's experience, agency, and voice. Attentive to production circumstances and the contexts of the respective films' emergence, the chapter provides insights into the originality and power of Armstrong's storytelling.

Due in part to generic characteristics of Armstrong's first feature *My Brilliant Career* in the risk-averse context of international commercial film production, Armstrong's reputation overseas has largely been built via the period drama: four of her five international feature films contain period film themes or are period film hybrids, and all refashion and recombine themes and elements from further genres to suit Armstrong's purposes. In the global cinema marketplace, period films are realist dramas set in the distant but still familiar past, which typically include an interest in modern and pre-modern technologies, pre-industrialised forms of day-to-day human activities such as employment and habitation, an approach to courtship, romance, and marriage which may both appear 'old-fashioned' and articulate present-day concerns, and an emphasis on costuming (Vidal 2012; Pidduck 2004). Regardless of production circumstances, period films tend to be marketed as arthouse in the US, though may carry representational burdens cut to a national agenda in cinemas such as Britain and Australia. Period films have proven capable of winning critical awards and been successful at the box office, but due to their presumed appeal to female audiences, have been vulnerable to critical denigration.[1]

Both critical literature and popular discussions of period films often note their Trojan Horsing of important and sometimes contentious issues through apparently light or conventional themes and events which may be deemed too simple or silly to warrant much attention. I would argue that through seemingly unimportant features Armstrong is able to smuggle in politically and socially significant themes concerning the repression of women's agency, women's ability to act independently from restrictive patriarchal authority, and women's potency as storytellers. Further issues Armstrong's international period movies explicitly refer to include class privilege (*Little Women*), capital punishment (*Mrs. Soffel*), and anti-Semitism (*Charlotte Gray*). As a result, the movies interestingly combine themes of social relevance with textual elements drawn from fantasy and romance.

Mrs. Soffel: confinement and the power of silence

As Armstrong's first dramatic feature made outside Australia, *Mrs. Soffel* (1984) offered a learning opportunity about commercial American film production and generally raised Armstrong's awareness about the positive and negative aspects of directing overseas. In interviews, Armstrong has stated that she found relations with MGM to be different from what she had anticipated and found herself having to fight for conditions that she thought had been agreed to, such as the number of days and locations permitted for the shoot (Shirley 2011). In the making of this movie, Armstrong became aware of her relative power and privilege as a non-American director in that she could afford to stand her ground and, if need be, even abandon a project and still have another country to which she could return and continue to make films.[2] Though a few minor factors conspired to produce a box office performance somewhat lower than Armstrong had hoped, e.g. a non-optimal Boxing Day release and publicity and marketing which fell short (Shirley 2011), the film attracted critical praise and remains one Armstrong is proud of.

Set in nineteenth-century Pittsburgh, *Mrs. Soffel* was inspired by the true story of a prison warden's wife who leaves her husband and young children for a charismatic prisoner on death row. A deeply religious woman, Kate Soffel (Diane Keaton) conspires to help Ed Biddle (Mel Gibson) and his brother Jack (Matthew Modine) escape and joins them on their ill-fated journey across the wintery, rural Pennsylvania landscape. Hunted down and ultimately captured by a posse in the end, Biddle and his brother are shot dead while Kate is taken into custody and back to the very same prison where the story began.

In generic terms, *Mrs. Soffel* has been recognised as a puzzle (Collins 1999: 41). The film has been compared to other historically set romances, including *The French Lieutenant's Woman* (MGM, 1981) and the romance-crime hybrid, *Bonnie and Clyde* (Warner Bros, 1967), indicating both the critical uncertainty over which box to place the film in and its borrowing of conventions from more than one genre (D'Erasmo 2002; Ebert 1984). Marketing for the film was built around a pair of blockbuster stars and aimed to capitalise on audiences' interest in their on-screen romance: Mel Gibson had just completed *The Year of Living Dangerously* (1982) and the pair of *Mad Max* movies (*Mad Max* (1979); *Mad Max 2* (1981)), and Diane Keaton was known to audiences through numerous Woody Allen movies and most recently *Reds* (1981). In story themes and cinematography (by Russell Boyd), *Mrs. Soffel* was a dark drama overlaid with issues of social justice and culminating in an unhappy end. Adding to the taxonomical and marketing challenges was the above-mentioned release of the film on Boxing Day and its badging as a Christmas film.

Armstrong claims that what first attracted her to the story was curiosity about the emotions driving Kate Soffel's decisions, namely why a middle-class, deeply religious woman would sacrifice so much to run off with a lowly prisoner (Shirley 2011). While many thought Biddle's motivations were instrumentalist,

Armstrong felt convinced that the love was mutual and reciprocated, citing the fact that the trio had stayed together long after it was practical to do so. It is possible that these convictions may have supported Armstrong's quest for authenticity in the depicted relationship between the two lead characters and positioned the film to explore what Collins referred to as the 'emotional truth' surrounding Mrs. Soffel's motivations (1999: 41). Scenes between Gibson and Keaton arguably go beyond familiar conventions to reveal the contextual and perhaps more authentic side of human relationships.

As Armstrong's first international feature, the film enabled the development and expansion of signature feminist and non-feminist themes named in this book's introduction; these include women's need to leave the confines of security and the domestic in order to become fully human, the ill effects on women of domination and oppression, and the positive value of the journey. Like *My Brilliant Career*, the film also gave voice to the class underdog, i.e. the two 'criminal' brothers. The film introduced new themes which hadn't been seen before, including the value of silence as a communicative medium, the pathologising of women who strive for independence, and the importance of women's self-determination of their own sexuality.

The movie opens on hazy shots of the Pittsburgh industrial skyline slowly brightening at daybreak. Conveyor belts move huge containers of materials, while men huddle on street corners around outdoor kettle fires. Shot in the blueish light of wintery dawn, the massive and imposing Allegheny County Jail comes into view. Large, geometric shapes of the building are depicted against the barely brightening sky, while the building's sheer enormity overwhelms those who stand in front of it.

The purpose of this short introductory sequence is clearly to intimate the brutality of the steel industry, the relentless pace of the work, and likely toll on human workers at the time when the story takes place. The building is crucial in this regard and was apparently the visual lure that producer Scott Rudin used to entice Armstrong to sign on-board; Armstrong was adamant about the requirement for on-location shooting, and it isn't hard to see why.[3] Built in 1888 by Henry Hobson Richardson, the building appears dehumanising on account of its sheer size and thus quickly and efficiently conveys the comparatively low value of working people's lives at this historical moment.

The camera pans from the top of the edifice down to the sidewalk, where tiny figures walk briskly past. As the titles conclude, three bodies kneel in front of the building and begin to prey, as the camera's attention drifts up to the barred windows behind which the prisoners are held. The image cuts to an extreme close up on a woman's eyes opening while a scream pierces the soundtrack. Kate Soffel awakens from a bad dream.

As a story which deals centrally with the minutiae of confinement and corresponding fantasies of escape, the movie takes steps to convey that imprisonment may take several forms, from the literal and corporeal to the emotional and psycho-sexual. In the film's logic, some forms of incarceration are more visible than others. Kate experiences immobility through the state of being bedridden and unwell, and her husband's unwillingness or inability to treat her as fully human is tantamount to punishment. Where Kate wishes to communicate with him in the movie's opening scene, Peter instead exhorts her to take medicine that will help her to sleep; later, he moves to call for the doctor when Kate, fully recovered, descends the staircase, hugs her children, and begins to interact playfully with them. Kate protests that the doctor 'never knew' what was wrong with her and casts doubt on his clinical abilities, while Peter expresses frustration at the sudden improvement in his wife's health. With evident exasperation he replies, 'How can anyone be ill for three months and suddenly get up one morning and say she's fine? It doesn't make sense.'

Although the opening titles of the movie state 'Pittsburgh 1901: A True Story' and we know that Ron Nyswaner's screenplay was based on real characters, the historical facts of the mental health of the real Kate Soffel are not known. What is clear is that the nineteenth-century American medical establishment considered women to be especially vulnerable to 'nervous troubles' or neurasthenia, a popular medical term used to describe 'a loss of "nerve energy" that could result in a host of symptoms including fatigue, vague bodily pains, melancholia, hysteria and even . . . a "lack of moral poise"' (Tsang 2015: 139).[4] While the vicissitudes of Kate's illness are not disclosed, they potentially fall within the 'wastepaper basket' of symptoms which are associated with hysteria (Surkis n.d.). Where nineteenth-century neurology saw women as victims of their own unruly bodies (and poor women's bodies especially invited containment and discipline), hysteria has been called an 'illness of being a woman in an era that strictly limited female roles' (Hustvedt 2011: 4). In the gendered environment of late nineteenth/early twentieth-century medicine, intimations of these illnesses and mental ill-health in general could be leveraged to circumscribe the legal rights and professional opportunities of even middle-class women, such as Kate Soffel (Nielsen 2019). In the logic of the story, Kate being ill both indicates her otherness and justifies her husband's controlling authority.

In scenes between Kate and Peter, this is often communicated via the *mise-en-scène*. The Victorian middle-class interiors are warmly lit yet ironically instruments of isolation, loneliness, regimentation, and paternally inflicted discipline. Peter's dismissal of his wife's ability to think for herself is shown in a scene when Kate publishes a letter against capital punishment, which Peter interprets as a sign that she needs a 'rest'. In a subsequent scene, Kate's moral opinion of the rectitude of capital punishment is constructed by Peter as 'sympathies' which she must 'control'.

While Kate's abilities appear limited from Peter's perspective, Kate is clearly at ease in the prison environment, in the company of prisoners, guards, and labourers. The direct cut, named above, to Keaton's face and voice following the opening shots of the prison exterior subtly implies an association between Kate and the prison inhabitants. Once shown moving around inside the prison walls, she greets workers with confidence and self-assurance, and her sure-footed and playful retort that the cleaner Lenny's going to church 'doesn't look like it did [him] much good' contrasts sharply with the subservience she displays with her husband. Although the prison is a thoroughly regimented place, Kate crosses its many and diverse spaces with ease and fluidity. In depicting this, the film builds a counterhegemonic fantasy about white middle-class women's potential allegiance with the underclass of prisoners, at odds with her husband's understanding of Kate's capacities and with other on-screen representations. While public discourse (in the form of newspaper headlines) characterises Kate's feelings for Ed as 'weak woman's insane infatuation', the immediate cut from these headlines to Ed staring intently at her, gives the lie to this construction and reveals that the affection is mutual and authentic.

In keeping with Armstrong's award-winning *My Brilliant Career*, *Mrs. Soffel* insists on the importance of telling the story from Kate's point of view; this is achieved via scripting and camera work and notably the strategic use of silence. Directly after the newspaper headline 'Biddles will hang' is cruelly revealed to Jack and Ed, Peter and Kate are shown sitting quietly at home. There is a slow tracking shot across a table of small mechanical parts, which Peter fiddles with. As he pauses and looks up at his wife, the camera pans slowly across to Kate on the other side of the table, her gaze initially fixed downwards, and her hand playing absent-mindedly around her lips with a wooden object, possibly a small spool. She appears anxious and lost in thought and she rolls the spool around with her fingertips. The shot is seventy-five seconds in length and ends with a close-up on Kate's face as she lowers the spool from her lips, comes to rest the edge of her chin on her curled fist, lifts and focuses her gaze, and appears to gain clarity of thought.

In *Film and Female Consciousness: Irigaray, Cinema and Thinking Women*, Lucy Bolton examines a set of arthouse movies directed by women which emphasise the self-explorations of lead female characters; according to Bolton, movies by Jane Campion, Sofia Coppola, and Lynne Ramsay offer a genuine alternative to commercial cinema's normative objectification of women and reduction of them to the status of an enigma (2011). Bolton claims that focusing on women's inner lives and processes of self-exploration may shift audiences' focus away from concerns with feminine appearance to fuller representations (2011: 3). Bolton writes: 'In this mode of filming it appears that the spectator is privy to the interiority of the female characters. ... I use the term "consciousness" to refer to the characters' inner lives, their thoughts, desires, fears, and emotions, and the introspective contemplation of these' (2011: 3). One of the means Bolton advocates to access this interiority is attention to silence: 'Silence and pauses, as opposed to dialogue, could convey interiority without perhaps requiring obvious articulation or representation: just as the spectator watches in silence, so they witness the woman on-screen experiencing self-reflection and repose' (2011: 51).

In the shot described above, silence offers such an inroad into Kate Soffel's inner thoughts. In concluding with a focus on Kate's face and showing a subtle shift in her frame of mind, the shot prioritises this character's perspective and repositions the silence she requires as the communicative norm within the scene. Depicting Kate's focus off-screen and away from her husband, the shot furthermore intimates the bankruptcy of the white middle-class matrimonial relationship.

In other scenes between the two, the relationship between Peter and Kate appears formal, unphysical, and characterised by heteronormative forms of submission and dominance. Kate often appears with downcast eyes, restrained and obedient in Peter's presence, while Peter seems either mystified by his wife's emotions or insistent on correcting them; in both cases it is clear that Peter condescendingly believes his wife is (unfortunately, inappropriately) ruled by emotions. For example, in a scene just after the children have been sent to stay with relatives prior to when the Biddles are to be hanged, Peter and Kate sit together alone in the dining room, isolated and divided in the formal Victorian home setting. Kate makes a final pitch to Peter for the two of them to go away; but it goes unheeded. 'It is a good position', Peter counters, in a delivery that concludes with a long and high shot. In this ending shot of the sequence, the two are positioned slightly off-centre (towards the top right of the frame) at a vast dining room table circled by empty chairs, as Keaton again falls silent.

In a film which spends considerable time revealing various tiers of masculinised power – male wardens, male prison guards, and male labourers outside – to recentre the story-telling around a single female protagonist requires a narrational and cinemato-graphic strategy which is both deliberate and concentrated and which offers an alternative to the powers of noise and voice that are elsewhere in the film. Though Keaton remains silent in the shot with the spool and grows quiet in the dining room scene, movements in her eyes and fingers subtly convey changes in her emotional state. In doing this, the scenes indicate a new means of communication and confer value on acts of silent interaction.

Place and escape

As a story which depicts Kate's move away from heteronorma-tive, repro-normative family life into independence and full subjecthood, *Mrs. Soffel* uses a range of largely exterior physical landscapes to depict Kate's growing independence and changes in her emotional circumstances. Consider the depiction of the break-out. After the trio depart the prison, a pair of shots (together less than twenty-five seconds in length) show the exterior of the prison, radically transformed by silently falling snow: the building is white-tinged and the street bears a six-inch cover, through which Jack Biddle playfully slides. Soon after, passage on a freight train allows a first glimpse of a snow-covered rural wilderness from Kate's point of view. In a way that appears joyous, the three of them project themselves from the train into the snow-covered terrain, as they jump. Later, in the dark, they make their way across a snow-covered field to an abandoned schoolhouse, where the cold bone-coloured walls of the interior and steel-blue colour of the snowy exterior resemble nothing seen previously in the movie. Jack and Ed source a sleigh and the trio head north to Canada at daybreak, when the colour of the scene is, again, steel-blue. Throughout these outdoor scenes, Ed, Kate, and Jack are frequently depicted with scant protection from the elements, with many shots showing their sleigh coming into view, and the only sound being the ringing of the sleigh bells.

Other post-escape scenes similarly take place in quiet, still, peaceful, and likewise snow-covered landscapes, or in brightly lit, simply furnished, rural homes; the latter offer a marked contrast with the heavy furnishings of the middle-class Victorian interiors shown in earlier moments in the film. The brightness of these scenes signals jubilant, never-before-felt emotions for Kate and the two escaped convicts and new opportunities for the expression of physicality and movement.

Sue Thornham is at the forefront of current-day theorising about the significance of place in contemporary women's filmmaking. Thornham takes as her point of departure for exploring the construction of place in stories helmed by women directors, Teresa de Lauretis's now landmark explication of 'hero' and 'space', written by de Lauretis at an early moment of feminist film theory (Thornham 2019: 7). In de Lauretis's formulation, the human components in well-known Western narratives are gendered as male, heroic, and active, while elements of place (including physical obstacles, boundaries, and portions of terrain) are gendered female. According to de Lauretis, quest narratives feature male heroes navigating space that is often feminised in order to become human, while the female remains 'an element of plot-space, a topos, a resistance, matrix and matter' (de Lauretis 1983: 119; quoted in Thornham 2019: 1).

In 1983 when these words were published, de Lauretis's attention to the semiotics of place marked a departure from the work of many of her contemporaries, who were used to relying on metaphors of vision and specularity to describe cultural inscriptions of gendered power relations; in so doing, de Lauretis presciently anticipated developments in theories of gender, spatiality, and landscape that would burgeon some twenty years later in research by Thornham, Guiliana Bruno (2002), and Elizabeth Grosz (1995).

Released just one year after the publication of *Alice Doesn't*, Armstrong's welding of Kate's liberation to notions of place imaginatively and productively re-contours the hegemonic semiotics of place outlined by de Lauretis and Thornham.[5] Evidence of Kate's freedom in these new spaces include Kate's throwing herself from the speeding train, her experiencing of enjoyable sex (in the brightly lit, modestly furnished farmhouse), and speaking on equal terms with a male partner, in the abandoned rural schoolhouse. While the Victorian interiors indicated entrapment for Kate, the rural spaces auger an opportunity to become more fully human.

In contrast to Kate's (and Ed's and Jack's) experiences, for the all-male hunting posse in search of the Biddles the wintery landscapes are something to be endured, traversed, and ultimately mastered in the process of the capture. As the posse grows in number and enthusiasm, the sound of the pursuing party becomes louder and more raucous, contrasting sharply with the sound of gentle sleigh bells heard in shots with Kate, Ed, and Jack. The posse of seven or eight hunters and their sleigh closes in. A high shot shows the posse only a few horse-lengths away. Ed is shot and falls to the bottom of the sleigh where his face and Kate's are captured in close-up. She says 'I can't go back', indicating that she too is now a fugitive, as Jack and Ed are. A shot rings out and Keaton collapses. Shortly after, another shot and Jack and Ed fall from the carriage. The party of now ten or fifteen men close in to kill Ed and Jack as they crawl away from the gun fire. The ending low-angled shot is from the point of view of the dying men, revealing seventeen solemn faces in close-up, standing in a circle and staring down in the direction of the camera; the final face shown staring at the Biddles belongs to a teenage boy. That the final shot shows this young face reveals the movie's understanding of conventionalised masculinity and its association of this with cruelty: in the logic of this scene, men travel in men-only packs, are devoid of mercy, and educate their youngest members to replicate such behaviour, perhaps as precondition to becoming men.

The film concludes with Kate being ushered to her cell, offered a bouquet of flowers by the prison maid, and ministered to by Agnes (a prison matron). The flowers recall the flowers in the poem read previously by Ed, suggesting there may be further women to support Kate during her incarceration, as she once offered support to Ed. The music swells, a smile creeps across Kate's face as she reads the poem Ed wrote for her earlier. Mel Gibson's voice fills the soundtrack: 'Just a little violet from across the way, came to cheer a prisoner in his cell one day. Just a little flower sent by a loving hand, has a kindly meaning that true hearts understand . . .' Positioned outside Kate's cell, the camera turns away from her and moves swiftly down the hallway with gathering speed. The movement and gently upbeat music convey exuberance that seems narratively out of step with ending events.

Music notwithstanding, what are we to make of Kate's incarceration, which concludes the movie, the only non-happy ending within the whole of Armstrong's commercial work, and largely out of step with the happy ending of popular romance? I believe it is important to pause and recognise the radical courage which must have been required on Armstrong's part to defend such an ending, which itself foregrounds women's insistence on achieving their aims without compromise. Armstrong has talked freely about studio pressure to include happy endings and recognised the artistic value when films do not end in such ways (Shirley 2011). Though Armstrong doesn't mention the larger politics attending such decisions, she doesn't need to. In the context of a powerful studio's decision-making ability, Armstrong's insistence on standing her ground now appears nothing less than a cinematic, industrial, and possibly even feminist triumph and deserves to be celebrated as such. As for the moderately upbeat concluding music, this brings a tonal contradiction and ambiguity to the scene and in so doing, an interpretative challenge that is also out of step with conventional generic romance endings. This largely unhappy ending, containing a kernel of hope conveyed by the music, Keaton's small smile, and the accelerated camera movement, suggests the abiding emphasis on the theme of women's independence, regardless of cost.

From *Fires Within* to *Little Women*

Armstrong's attachment to her next American commercial project came about through her interest in an original script about Cuban exiles in Miami, by Cuban-American Cynthia Cidre. *Fires Within* is a contemporary-set drama with political undertones about a Cuban political prisoner named Nestor Varona (played by Jimmy Smits). Nestor is released from prison, leaves Cuba, and goes to join his wife Isabel (played by Greta Scacchi) from whom he has been separated for eight years. While Nestor was incarcerated in a Cuban prison, Isabel was able to leave Cuba with their daughter on a flimsy raft and join the Cuban-American community in Miami. Thinking Nestor was unlikely ever to escape, Isabel took an American lover in Nestor's absence, Sam (Vincent D'Onofrio). The film is essentially a love triangle about what happens after Nestor arrives.

Critics of Armstrong's work have tended to avoid discussion of this film, which Armstrong herself has referred to as a 'turkey' (Shirley 2011). While Armstrong was drawn to the project by the story of personal challenge confronting someone who has to choose between their political beliefs and their family, the project was beset with challenges, stemming in part from what Armstrong found to be an inexperienced production team (Wallis Nacita and Lauren Lloyd) who in the end were unable to defend her vision. Casting for the project was challenging (in particular casting for the part of rejected lover Sam), there were negative responses in pre-screenings, the studio panicked, and the film was ultimately turned over to a different editing team for a complete re-cut.[6] The result was a film from which Armstrong asked to have her name removed, with little of the movie's original content. The central premise, about having to choose between political beliefs and family, bears a vague resemblance to themes seen previously in *My Brilliant Career* (and which would appear ten years later in *Charlotte Gray* (2001)), but overall the status of *Fires Within* on Armstrong's CV remains nebulous and it is difficult to determine where it fits in Armstrong's 'oeuvre'.

Little Women

An adaptation of the American literary classic by Louisa May Alcott, *Little Women* revisits themes seen in Armstrong's other commercial genre movies, including women's independence, the obligations and benefits of family, and strong, iconoclastic female characters who are at odds with social constraints. There are significant differences between *Mrs. Soffel* and *Little Women* in the meaning and images ascribed to home and family, in particular. In the patriarch-dominated world of *Mrs. Soffel*, home is a place of repression and subjugation; in the homosocial world of *Little Women*, it is largely a source of strength and love. Where family in *Mrs. Soffel* is the site of women's oppression and imposed hierarchy, family in *Little Women* is elevated in importance, even above the status of the heterosexual couple (Cobb 2015).

Little Women has been Armstrong's most successful commercial studio feature film to date. The film was distributor Sony's second top-grossing picture in 1994, the most commercially lucrative movie helmed by a woman that year, and one of the highest-grossing woman-directed Hollywood movies of the decade.[7] The commercial importance of Armstrong's achievement with *Little Women* cannot be emphasised enough. While a handful of women directors had achieved commercial success in the early 1990s – Penny Marshall with *A League of Their Own* (1992) and Nora Ephron with *Sleepless in Seattle* (1993) – at the time of *Little Women*, generational contemporaries of Armstrong were still working in largely low budget and independent spheres; Kathryn Bigelow's experience extended to a couple of independent features each of which had grossed less than $10 million and Mimi Leder had not yet directed the pair of action films that would make substantial amounts of money (*The Peacemaker* (1997) and *Deep Impact* (1998)). For women, the pathway to wide-release commercial studio features was still quite narrow: advocacy movements and associated ideas like #Time's Up and inclusion riders were still far off in the future.

Armstrong's third feature directed in the United States, *Little Women* provided the director with the opportunity to work under conditions that were vastly more supportive than she had experienced with *Fires Within*. Armstrong was able to partner with a strategic and experienced production team with demonstrated passion for the project who were surehanded about everything, including the all-important issues of marketing and release. Armstrong was approached to direct *Little Women* by Denise Di Novi, who had established a successful track record producing *Batman Returns* (1992) as well as films for Tim Burton. Armstrong initially rejected the invitation to become involved as she felt that the story repeated a number of the themes she had already dealt with in *My Brilliant Career*, but because of a mix of circumstantial factors (a different project which fell through at the last minute; Di Novi's persistence), Armstrong eventually agreed to meet with Di Novi, writer Robin Swicord, and Winona Ryder, who had already signed with the project. In this early phase, Armstrong developed a vision for how Ryder could embody the character Jo in new ways and discovered that the film was backed by Amy Beth Pascale, an experienced executive producer 'with clout', who had been named after not one but two *Little Women* characters (Shirley 2011). On the basis of these auspicious factors, Armstrong signed on to the project.

The story was shot in Deerfield, Massachusetts and in Vancouver over the course of several seasons to mirror the complex duration of the book's unfolding events. Armstrong's pre-production process was wide-ranging and encompassed, among other things, research into the time period when the story was set, Alcott's family biography, the transcendentalist movement, and even scarlet fever. Armstrong made an effort to determine the reasons for the book's enduring popularity (it is worth noting that the novel has never gone out of print since the year of its publication) and came to feel in the course of her research that Alcott's honesty and lack of sentiment in depicting the sisters' relationships played a pivotal role; her goal was to emphasise relationships, emotions, and humour, to populate the films with three-dimensional characters, and to capture a sense of what it is truly like to be sisters.

Armstrong has spoken generously about the cast and crew she was privileged to work with and about the genuine warmth and friendships that developed between cast members; her assertion is that these friendships translate into the on-screen relationships.[8] Casting included established stars Susan Sarandon as Marmee and Ryder as Jo, actors who had acted in smaller roles or on television, such as Christian Bale as Teddy and Trini Alvarado as Meg, and relative newcomers Claire Danes (Beth) and the young Kirsten Dunst (Amy). Casting also included actors with whom Armstrong had worked previously (Trini Alvarado had appeared as one of the Soffel children in *Mrs. Soffel*).

Because of the confluence of factors – the movie's adapting of a well-known and much loved literary classic, its on-screen treatment of women's authorship, and not least its box office success – there has already been considerable scholarly attention to the movie's advancing of feminist themes, including its prioritising of women's agency and wisdom and representation of a self-sufficient female household and feminist politics more generally (Cobb 2015; Rueschmann 2000). The updating of the nineteenth century story for contemporary times has also been pointed out: Armstrong and writer Swicord largely abandoned the morality components of Alcott's novel which stressed young women's pursuit of self-improvement through apprehension of 'Christian virtues of self-denial and self-sacrifice' (Rueschmann 2000: 27).

The most prevalent mechanism at Armstrong's/Swicord's disposal to engage contemporary audiences is the playful rewriting or overturning of gender roles in ways that run somewhat counter to heteronormative masculinity and femininity. With the exception of one brief moment when Teddy proposes to Jo, Jo and Teddy's relationship is a compelling exception to the heteronormative male-female relationship seen in nearly all commercial popular romances at this time. From the moment audiences first see him, Teddy appears baffled by gender codes. He claims his ignorance of the 'rules' of heterosexual courtship is the reason why he hides behind a curtain at a dance where Jo accidentally stumbles upon him. When later Amy expresses surprise that Jo is becoming friends with a *boy*, Jo counters he's not a boy, he's *Laurie*.

Throughout most of the movie, Laurie's non-participation in normative gender practices functions as a foil to showcase Jo's own lack of gender compliance. When he does dance with her shortly after meeting her behind the curtain, his hesitation provides an opening for Jo's more energetic movements, her taking of the man's dancing role, and lament that he does not know the 'lady's part'. Prone to class as well as gender pressure from his grandfather to go into business, later in the movie Teddy criticises the confluence of gender and class that would require him to go into one of the 'serious professions' and avoid the arts, here coded as feminine. He claims that his grandfather 'wants me in an office. Why is it Amy can paint, you can scribble away, while I must manfully set my music aside?'

The time frame of the movie's making in the early 1990s is now recognised as an important moment for the emergence of post-feminism: a performatively feminine, pro-sex, occasionally pro-queer stance which overtly rejected second-wave feminism's downplaying of gender difference in favour of a more fluid, playful, celebratory approach. By 1994, multiplex audiences were beginning to encounter muscular women stars like Linda Hamilton (in *Terminator 2: Judgement Day* (1991)), celebrated for her queering of the action genre (Ross 2009); within the next few years audiences would see further gender bending from other high-profile stars Geena Davis (*Long Kiss Goodnight* (1996)) and Demi Moore (*G. I. Jane* (1997)). In 1994 audiences might also have seen Madonna (in *Truth or Dare* (1991)) or Tilda Swinton (in *Orlando* (1992)). The point is that roles for women within popular culture at the moment when *Little Women* was released were undergoing rapid, dramatic changes that allowed for expressions of androgyny and queerness in new ways. *Little Women*'s playful approach to gender must be understood in this context.

Across all of Armstrong's movies, Jo is perhaps her queerest hero. Throughout the first three-quarters of the film up until her move to New York, Jo voices strong objections to feminine dress ('blast these wretched skirts'), compulsory matrimony, and even a desire for violence; she claims a desire to be like her father and go to war. In such moments, Jo's gender expression appears an authentic manifestation of both her personhood and an effect of her creative imagination, as evidenced in moments when she and her sisters perform in drag as characters from *The Pickwick Papers*. At these moments in the story, Jo's approach to creativity is aligned with the fantastical and the unknown, which she celebrates. She overtly counsels Beth 'never to write what you know', delights in making up stories about the new neighbour, Laurie, claims to have 'ten stories in my head right now', and owns those stories as friends: 'Late at night my mind would come along with voices and stories and friends as dear to me as any in the real world.' Imagination is fundamentally important to her, as evidenced through her successful publication of stories full of lunatics, vampires, and with titles like 'The Sinner's Corpse'.

Armstrong's belief in the creative potency of women's imagination aligns with a long line of scholars of popular culture, from Janice Radway (1984) to Teresa de Lauretis (1994), both of whom have identified the power and potency of fantasy for women audiences and readers. Unanimous amongst feminist scholars of popular culture is an understanding of the critical and strategic advantages for women in moving from fantasy's object to becoming its creators and consumers. In terms of the film *Little Women*, 'creators' include director Armstrong, author Alcott, and scriptwriter Robin Swicord, in addition to the fictional character Jo.

Home: locus of resistance

While Jo spends much of the time aligned in these ways and there is considerable pleasure for audiences in viewing these aspects, by the end of the story the film must transform her into a willing conscript within regimes of compulsory heterosexuality and alter her writing into a more 'authentic' expression, as stipulated by her lover, Friedrich. Because of a few factors – Friedrich not being a conventional patriarch; the consolidation of Jo's authorship in the form of a published manuscript – it has been argued that marriage will not compromise Jo's feminist identity (Cobb 2015: 89–90). I am in agreement with Cobb on this and believe that the movie offers one more device to serve as a bulwark against the restrictions and limitations that would otherwise arrive with the event of conventional hetero-patriarchal marriage, which is the concept of *home*. Although Jo's and her sisters' marital statuses undergo change over the story's course, home is the constant which does not change very much. Home is a metonym for family, which is itself identified with a form of love that is opposed to heterosexual matrimony. As Amy exclaims, a sister is 'a relation stronger than marriage'.

Many of the March sisters voice a longing for the idea of home and appreciation of the beauty of its physical iteration. Beth exclaims when descending the staircase after her first bout of illness, 'the house is beautiful'; Amy exclaims that she 'went to Europe to paint the great cathedrals but couldn't get home out of my [her] mind'. Participation with the family, in the home, requires staying close, and there are exhortations amongst the sisters not to go so far away. Jo says to Amy, 'Promise me that you'll always live close by; I couldn't bear losing another sister.' Moving away is nearly equated with death, as when Beth (on her deathbed) says, 'Why does everyone want to go away? I love being home. But I don't like being left behind. Now I'm the one going ahead.'

The significance of home is established visually via numerous interior shots (devised in collaboration with cinematographer Geoffrey Simpson). Many of these contain multiple characters in movement, requiring extensive blocking and complex cho-reography. Many of these sequences end in a kind of static tableau, framing the quartet of sisters with Marmee, often settled on each other's laps, generally facing outwards to the camera. The opening scene illustrates this. The March children flock to their returning mother to gather around and to hear her read aloud a letter from their absent father. There are five shots in the sequence; in the sixth, little Amy is settled on her mother's lap, with sisters directly behind and on either side, and Marmee framed in the middle. The camera takes forty seconds to track in to a close-up framing all five characters facing outwards, before the image cuts to an exterior shot looking at the cuddling family from the frosty exterior of the window. The Christmas carol 'Ding Dong Merrily on High' starts on the soundtrack and forms a sound bridge to the next scene, of the characters gathered around the piano.

Framing and camera movements such as these accomplish several things. Most obviously, they depict the family as physically and emotionally close, the home as physically and emotionally 'warm', and Marmee as the emotional and physical centre. The sequence creates a conceptual association between the emotional qualities of 'family' and the graphic shape of the tableau and further situates that image within the physical setting of the house interior. The family tableau shots only appear in the March home; outside the home family members are more likely to appear in two-shots with their respective beloveds, or in crowd-shots (in the boarding house in New York, for example, or in the neighbour's home as Meg prepares for the coming-out party). The number of characters assembled in the tableau shot (all five women in the family) and the stillness of the camera centring on them, is both unique to the house and the family group and contrasts with other social arrangements and framings, such as the wedding party's circling of the wedding pole.

Cinematographically, establishing shots of the home's exterior function as punctuation points marking the conclusion of scenes and alerting audiences to turns in the narrative. The film opens on a series of atmospheric shots of 'Concord, Mass': a tree fallen in the snow, a portion of a post and rail fence, a wreath being hung on a door, a Christmas tree being pulled down the street. After these shots, the house in its entirety is shown, followed by the greeting scene with Marmee, followed by another exterior shot of the house. A shot of the home concludes the film, spied by the camera as it rises from a shot of Jo and Friedrich kissing.

Assisted via exterior shots of the house such as these, the March home (the historically named 'Orchard House') becomes the visual and physical anchor for all the most important family activities. Most positive story events take place in the home; these include the playing out of scenes from *The Pickwick Papers*, Jo's writing in the attic, the greeting of Marmee when she returns, several singing events by the piano, and Beth's receiving the piano as a gift. Outside the home, events are more treacherous: Beth contracts scarlet fever, Meg's marriage (which Jo disdains) to John is carried out, Teddy's misguided proposal to Jo is uttered, and various balls and coming-out parties are attended which Jo at least doesn't enjoy. The home is the place of childhood relations and sisterly warmth, which are prioritised highly.

In addition to being positioned on the cusp of a wave of post-feminist expressions as mentioned earlier, the film's release date (1994) coincided with the founding date for the media technology giants Yahoo and Amazon. Social media behemoths Myspace and Facebook would arrive a mere nine and ten years later and, with their arrival, irrevocably transform middle-class homes like that depicted in *Little Women* and in other popular movies like *Home Alone* (1990) into places of ostensible social fragmentation, withdrawal, and isolation. Some of *Little Women's* success is due to its release at a historical time when 'home' was still able to be construed as a positive. Through Armstrong's cinema at this point in time, 'home' can be a powerful place of community, refuge, and benefit for women friends, sisters, mothers, and daughters.

Armstrong in Europe: popular films after the year 2000

In the 2000s Armstrong gained new opportunities to direct feature films in France, Scotland, and England. Both *Charlotte Gray* (2001) and *Death Defying Acts* (2007) received funding from a range of UK, Australian, and German sources; the strategies employed by Armstrong at this moment were in step with changes in policy mechanisms and support structures which came into view after 2000. As Ryan and Goldsmith note, '[t]he period between 2000 and 2015 has been defined by a marked international turn in Australian film and television production, as well as the internationalisation of policy mechanisms and industry support structures designed to support a national production system' (2017: 2).

Transnational cinema is a critical concept which takes its definition from a range of textual and industrial factors including authorship, stardom, modes of production and exhibition; some scholars employ a deliberately broad definition in order to avoid accusations of essentialism (Shaw and De La Garza 2010). Research into transnational cinema sometimes posits a developmental teleology where cinema movements and individual auteurs are said to progress from the national to the transnational (Ezra and Rowden 2006; Higson 2006). While Armstrong slots into that narrative in that her Hollywood movies preceded her forays into multinationally financed filmmaking and exhibits a transnationalism in her approach (particularly to scripting and casting), her authorship confounds any such progressional interpretation, in the interweaving of Australian work (*Unfolding Florence* (2006); *Love, Lust & Lies* (2010); *Women He's Undressed* (2015)) in and around her transnational feature films.

Charlotte Gray is a World War Two-era romantic thriller about a Scotswoman, Charlotte Gray, who parachutes behind enemy lines in France to join the French Resistance and search for her lost RAF-pilot lover; once in France, she meets and falls in love with a communist member of the Resistance, Julien Lavade. In the logic of the story, Charlotte's participation in the Resistance is not without challenges. In an early scene, she appears to contribute to the exposure of a female colleague and her subsequent removal by collaborationist French forces; in a later scene she is accused by Julien of delivering information which may have precipitated an attack on some Resistance friends. Though Charlotte turns out not to be culpable, the allegations of such misdeeds contribute to a construction of Charlotte as mysterious, and her activities as potentially ineffective or even harmful. The movie makes subtle comparisons between Charlotte's activities and those of Julien, implying that she traffics in smaller scale forms of resistance.

Adapted by Belgian-born, UK-based scriptwriter Jeremy Brock from a bestseller by British novelist Sebastian Faulks, *Charlotte Gray* bears a resemblance to real-time events and careers of French/British Special Operations Executive agent Violet Szabo and Australian Nancy Wake. While the story does not refer directly to either women's story, Armstrong has indicated that research she undertook in preparation for the film involved meeting one ex-SOE member who described personal experiences similar to what Charlotte undergoes (including jumping from a plane and falling in love). Although the film takes the form of a love story, I argue that it successfully brings a number of pertinent political themes to the table, such as the nature of women's resistance in wartime and the gendering of the French Resistance, and that it supports post-2000 fantasies of Europeanisation, largely via its Europeanising of the Holocaust (Erhart 2018: 98–101).

Armstrong's last period film, *Death Defying Acts* (2007), is a mother-daughter caper film with comedic and romantic elements, set in the world of magical theatrical entertainment in Edinburgh in the nineteen-teens and nineteen twenties. *Death Defying Acts* tells the story of the relationship between a fictional mother-daughter pair of clairvoyants and the American historical figure Harry Houdini, whom they aim to con.

From the film's perspective, 'magic' is a broad term and includes everything from the simplest sleights of hand and the disappearing of coins, to the shonky calling up of deceased love ones in public seances, to the blockbuster, high-quality physical feats that Houdini performs. The film compares and contrasts the varying forms of labour in high and low entertainment forms: high entertainment is clearly what Houdini practises, in touring the major capitals of the world, with the assistance of his businessman and minder, Mr Sugarman; low is practised by

Mary McGarvie and her daughter, Benji; Mary and Benji are the top-billed act at the local tent show, McTavish's Palace.

The distinctions between 'high' and 'low' are reproduced in the physical spaces the two acts respectively occupy and where they take place. While Houdini works his magic dramatically high above a crowd, out over the harbour, or up on stage, some of which is made apparent to *Death Defying*'s audiences via stylised, slow-motion close-ups, Benji has to scour the ground around the busy and bustling city sidewalks to prepare for their act, while Mary has to walk out on to a modelling catwalk to serve her audience.

The dichotomy between the fakery that Mary and Benji practise and the seemingly more high-quality endurance feats that Houdini performs maps furthermore on to the respective performers' personality traits and characteristics. Where Mary and Benji are aligned with the frivolous, the marginal, and the superficial, Houdini associates himself with the deep sobriety of the scientific community; he subscribes to the *Scientific American* and insists he wants to foster a true 'science experiment'.

In an attempt to further consolidate these divisions and expose Mary and Benji as fakes, Houdini offers a reward for anyone who is able to make contact with his dead mother and reveal her final words. The pair break into Houdini's quarters but cannot find evidence of the words. Houdini finds out and prepares to reveal them for what they are, when Benji begins to shake, shudder, and make the contact he seeks. In the movie's logic, this final performance is no fake; Benji, the film declares, has a real gift.

At first glance, the similarities between the two films appear quite slight, apart from the fact that both received international financing and both faced pre-production and production challenges.[9] Looked at more closely, however, the two movies contain a number of interesting overlaps. At the inception of each film is an international journey undertaken by one of the respective leading characters: the American Houdini has arrived in Scotland, and the Scotswoman Charlotte leaves for France; these movements are depicted textually (through the respective stories) and echoed paratextually through script and casting. Casting for the respective films stretched and extended the stories in interesting ways. In *Death Defying Acts*, the American Houdini was played by Australian actor Guy Pearce, with the roles of the mother-daughter Scottish clairvoyants performed by Welsh-born Catherine Zeta-Jones and Irish/American actor Saoirse Ronan, respectively. In *Charlotte Gray*, the Scottish operative was played by the Australian Cate Blanchett while Charlotte's French lover, Julien, was played by American actor Billy Crudup. In scripting, Armstrong's *Charlotte Gray* made one significant change to Faulks's original novel. Where in the novel Charlotte returns to Britain at the end of the story to rejoin her RAF-pilot lover, in the film she returns to London and finds the pilot but rejects him and makes a decision to return to France to join Julien. Thus the Scottish-English affair which concludes the novel becomes in the movie a Scottish-French union. Elsewhere I have argued that this script change anticipated pro-European sentiments in Britain at that time (2018: 101).

In addition to innovations in casting and scripting, significantly from the perspective of the approach canvassed by this book, both films characterise their lead female characters as mercurial performers; and both films celebrate these qualities and the specifically gendered forms of labour that the respective women perform.

Charlotte Gray and Mary McGarvie each depend for their livelihood on performances of masquerade or artifice: in Charlotte's case, she performs being French; in Mary's case, she pretends to be psychic and in contact with the dead. Early scenes in both films emphasise the women perfecting these abilities, and in both cases, audiences are in on the fake while diegetic audiences in the respective story worlds are not. Both films are alike in situating each woman at the low end of a gendered labour hierarchy. Both Charlotte and Julien are engaged in fighting fascism; both Mary and Houdini create magical entertainment. But where Julien's labour is constructed as virile and agentic, and Houdini's is venerated and respected as mentioned above, the women's labour, in both cases, is associated with considerably smaller successes, occasional misfires, and misinterpretation.

A central task that both films seek to accomplish by their respective conclusions is the overhauling and revising of these gendered conceptions of labour. By the end of *Death Defying Acts*, one half of the two-person, mother-daughter team – namely daughter Benji – has proven herself in possession of genuine magical abilities. By the conclusion of *Charlotte Gray*, the value of Charlotte's contributions is conveyed in a scene which shows her typing and then delivering a letter to two Jewish boys just as they are taken away. In both cases, Armstrong sheds new light on women's capacity to act in challenging circumstances, revises audience understanding of the labour women perform, and the gendered hierarchies in which they are all too often enmeshed.

Conclusion

Armstrong's long-standing and unwavering interest in commercial film forms was not always in step with what feminist film activists and theorists called for. The release of Armstrong's first big international commercial feature in 1984 (*Mrs. Soffel*) came at a time when Laura Mulvey's famous anti-Hollywood polemic, 'Visual Pleasure and Narrative Cinema' (1975) held tremendous currency. It is worth remembering that Mulvey concluded her article with what now appears a polemical call to arms against mainstream commercial genre film of exactly the type Armstrong was making: 'It is said that analysing pleasure or beauty annihilates it. That is the intention of this article' (Mulvey 1990: 30).

Forty-five years after the publication of Mulvey's essay, feminist media researchers are reappraising once overlooked forms and how women working in commercial genres utilise them to fashion stories with resonance for women audiences (Harrod and Paszkiewicz 2018; Thornham 2019; Paszkiewicz 2018). Several recent books explore what women stand to gain by working in film cycles or genres to extend, subvert, and sometimes overturn them. Mary Harrod and Katarzyna Paszkiewicz (2018) consider how women 'do' genre – how they revise and leverage generic components such as character, script, and setting to create new understandings and new forms of engagement and entertainment, often, but not solely, for the benefit of female audiences (see also Paszkiewicz 2018). Other research interrogates critics' rigidity and failure to understand the generically intersectional or hybrid films that women sometimes make and their tendency to exclude women from genre studies (Jermyn 2018; Erhart 2018). Throughout these interventions, scholars are looking at how movie authors negotiate their own positioning with respect to the gendered genres in which they work.

As an early proponent of commercial forms, Armstrong deserves to be key to these discussions. In spite of Armstrong's clear-cut affection for the Australian screen industry, there is no doubt about her ability to act effectively in international contexts, to bring a spectrum of talent together from around the globe, and to tell complex stories with transnational relevance.

Notes

1 The gendered assumptions of critics and theorists of historical films and related subgenres has been noted. See Pidduck (2004); Polaschek (2013); and Erhart (2018).
2 Armstrong has waxed proud about the smaller budget yet robustly cinephilic Australian filmmaking climate, where people work for less money but do so from love of cinema. Americans, Armstrong found, were required to focus on where they would obtain their next job. See Shirley 2011.
3 As the prison was still a working site, Armstrong was granted twenty-four hours on location to film, without any break, with the prisoners serving as extras (Shirley 2011).
4 Tsang is quoting early twentieth-century American medical expert Dr Samuel McComb (1910), 'Nervousness – A National Menace', *Everybody's Magazine*, 22, pp. 259–60.
5 Thornham canvasses a range of cinema and cultural theorists for new approaches to space, only to discover that the 'division proposed is inherently unequal and implicitly gendered. For Western literary theory,

argues W. J. T. Mitchell, space is "static, visual, external, empty, corporeal, and dead ... it must be pushed into motion, temporalized, internalized, filled up, or brought to life by time and consciousness" (1989: 93–4)' (Thornham 2019: 10).

6   According to Armstrong, after the test screening, she and the original editor were more or less kicked off the project and the film was handed to a different editor (Lou Lombardo) to be completely recut (Shirley 2011).

7   *Little Women* grossed $50 million and was outpaced by just three American woman-directed movies in the 1990s: *A League of Their Own* (Penny Marshall, 1992; lifetime gross $107 million), *Sleepless in Seattle* (Nora Ephron, 1993; lifetime gross $126 million), and *The Prince of Tides* (Barbra Streisand, 1991; lifetime gross $74 million). Note: it also outpaced *The Piano* (Jane Campion, 1993) by approximately $10 million.

8   Ryder went so far as to provide Armstrong with casting ideas: according to Armstrong, it was her suggestion that Christian Bale and Claire Danes be considered (Shirley 2011).

9   Regarding *Charlotte Gray*, Armstrong has described pre-production deliberations about language. While Armstrong was prepared to film in French, including sourcing French actors, translating the script, directing via an interpreter, and having Blanchett voice the dialogue in French as appropriate, the studio, Warner Bros, did not agree (Shirley 2011). Regarding *Death Defying Acts*, Armstrong has explained how an unexpected hole in the budget for the film caused a cascading set of problems which the film never quite recovered from (Shirley 2011). According to Armstrong, shooting time was radically curtailed and critical elements cut; the movie was furthermore inaccurately marketed to Harvey Weinstein, who was disappointed when it did not generically conform as he had been led to expect it would (Shirley 2011).

3

An Australian genre cinema: *My Brilliant Career, Oscar and Lucinda, Starstruck*

Australian genre movies have historically faced formidable challenges in achieving global popularity. This is due in no small part to the relative scale of production which in the case of Australian films is vastly smaller on average than that of most commercial Hollywood genre movies with which Australian movies have to compete. From 2010 to 2017, over half of Australian feature films were shot for less than $3 million (Screen Australia); in contrast, the average budget for a Hollywood movie at this time was $71 million (Quinn 2014). While Australian franchise movies such as *Happy Feet* obviously can (and have) become box office mega-performers, the box office performance of self-evidently 'Australian' films – films shot on location in Australia, featuring actors with recognisable Australian accents – are far less likely to succeed on the global stage. As Stuart Cunningham explains, the industry developed to trade in 'culturally specific films, dealing in recognisable Australian realisms, which authenticate and affirm Australian concerns ... or else internationalised films, geared to a culturally undifferentiated market' (Cunningham 1985: 235). Or as Mary Anne Reid articulates, 'Cultural difference, diversity, and the prioritisation of "Australian stories" is Australian film's "natural armour" against Hollywood dominance' (Reid 1999: 11; Reid is quoted in Ryan and Goldsmith 2017: 3).

Cunningham and Reid are writing from a historical standpoint that is obviously in the past and an ideological standpoint which would appear to be behind us, nonetheless there is evidence that the tension surrounding Australian cinema's essential 'Australian-ness', what counts as an Australian film, and what Australian films ought to be like, remains unresolved. Writing more recently, Mark David Ryan articulates that conflicts between the commercial requirements of most genre movies and the cultural mandates that were formulated at the beginning of the 1970s still haunt the Australian industry (Ryan 2012: 141).

Australian cinema is of course not any one thing and has undergone several major shifts in definition, iteration, and means of funding since the renaissance of the 1970s. The contributions of genre films to Australian cinema history have waxed and waned, with certain industrial moments privileging more robust engagements with popular genre cinema, than others. In the end, the most satisfying definition of current-day Australian cinema is a comprehensive one that takes into account its plethora of industrial strains. These include transnational narratives which are shot overseas and which barely mention Australia (*Lore; Moulin Rouge!; The Great Gatsby*); outward-looking Australian stories with intersections into international spaces (like *The Sapphires*); and movies with largely local relevance (such as *Red Dog* and *The Dressmaker*) (Ryan and Goldsmith 2017: 3).

The story of Armstrong's cinematic success is closely yoked to the history of the national industry. Armstrong's career begins when the Australian industry rebegins: with the 1970s Revival. As described in Chapter 1, Armstrong was supported through new initiatives to join the first cohort in the new national film school (AFTS) and went on to make her first feature with government assistance, from the New South Wales Film Corporation.[1] Armstrong's second feature film was a beneficiary of the new funding scheme called the 10BA,[2] and over the years Armstrong has continued to gain opportunities through other state-based initiatives. Symbiotically, she now lends her name to pro-industry initiatives such as the 'Make It Australian' campaign.

Chapter 2 articulated Armstrong's innovations across the space of international genre films. This chapter hones and extends those concerns to consider how her domestically produced popular works refashion generic component from a feminist point of view, and to bring a feminist perspective to the telling of recent and colonial-era Australian histories, with which her popular Australian films are centrally involved. The chapter considers how generic elements in Armstrong's two Australian-set period movies dovetail with developments around race and gender to render history in an affecting way and how the youth-oriented, pro-queer movie *Starstruck* blends themes from the backstage musical with Australian elements.

Genre, globally

From the perspective of global film production, the deployment of genre extends far beyond the boundaries of Hollywood and into the cinemas of India, Italy, Hong Kong, and elsewhere. The initial Hollywood-centrism of much genre criticism produced by academics, has broadened to consider the effects of transnational production on generic codes and marketing campaigns and the hybridising of aesthetics in an international space. There is now a robust and nuanced body of literature on international iterations of genres once considered exclusively American and on the influence of indigenous global genres on American movies (Oliete-Aldea et al. 2015; Gustafsson and Kääpä 2015; Dibeltulo and Barrett 2018).

Outlining the 'circuit of acknowledgements' between filmmakers and audiences, David Desser (2012: 640), reveals noir's glocal genealogy in contexts which include Japan and Hong Kong and the influence of these movies on American noir and neo-noir forms since World War Two (Desser 2012: 631). In doing this Desser recognises the influence of non-American output without fundamentally destabilising or overturning American-centric understandings.

Taking a crossover cross-cultural approach to the Australian Indigenous musical *The Sapphires*, Therese Davis (2014) explores that film's construction of 'minority' and 'mainstream' within both the diegetic world of the Vietnam era-set story and extratextually as a product of a unique Indigenous-majority production context. In contrast to many generic approaches which place American culture at the centre and depict the bringing of 'stories, histories and sensibility of a cultural minority or "other" into the mainstream', *The Sapphires* shows 'how minority cultural groups bring global cultural genres into their worlds and for their ends' (602). Davis thus shifts the discussion from the adding-of-difference to American genre forms to a consideration of how US culture is updated and utilised for local or minority ends. Periphery is remade to become the centre in the representational and production contexts she describes.

Period film and the Australian industry

In the history of Australian film, period movies occupy a central if somewhat contested place. A full decade before the release of *A Room with a View* (1985), the production that made Merchant Ivory a household name in the UK, and twenty years prior to the release of *Sense and Sensibility* (1995), the first of what became a decade's worth of Austenian fare, Australian period films emerged as a keystone in the newly fledged Australian film industry, aka the Australian Revival. The value of these movies within the 'new' cinema has been documented: period films reflected the commercial and aesthetic ambitions of the Australian Film Commission (AFC), the overseeing government body at the time and were leveraged to grant seriousness to the industry, both domestically and overseas (Dermody and Jacka 1988; Turner 1989; Rayner 2000; Elliott 2010).[3] Period films were thus enlisted in the service of the national cinema campaign and called on to articulate relevant national histories and heritages. As in the UK, Australian period movies traded in culturally relevant themes, like Australia's distinctness from other countries, typically the United States and the United Kingdom, and brought recognition to the fledging industry on the global stage. They were popular with domestic audiences and provided a small but vital number of opportunities for local auteurs to become known, both at home and internationally (Turner 1989).

In ideological terms, period films are backwards-looking fantasies which tend to map present day concerns on to historical events, and Armstrong's movies are no exception in this regard. Period films may be judged according to perceptions about their politics around ongoing matters about nation, race, gender, and belonging. Armstrong's *My Brilliant Career* and *Oscar and Lucinda* have both been interpreted to be entangled with such debates. In the time leading up to *My Brilliant Career*, agitation for women's rights led to significant outcomes including the Conciliation and Arbitration Commission's granting of equal pay for equal work (in 1972) and the Maternity Leave Act (passed in 1973); critical discussions of *Brilliant Career* often allude to such events. Eighteen years later, *Oscar and Lucinda*'s release followed landmark legal and human rights developments. These included the 1992 concluding of the ten-year-long Mabo court case, which found the concept of *terra nullius* to be an illegitimate myth and acknowledged Aboriginal and Torres Strait Islander peoples' ongoing connection with the land, and the 1996 release of the National Inquiry into the Separation of Aboriginal and Torres Strait Islander Children from their Families, entitled 'Bringing Them Home'. Both of these events made significant contributions to a cultural recasting of venerated colonial-era activities of exploration and discovery as invasion; Felicity Collins and Therese Davis credit the 1992 Mabo decision for bringing about a paradigm shift in how the nation thought of its own colonial past and the legitimacy of white settlement (2004). Discussions of *Oscar and Lucinda* have explicitly situated it in the context of Mabo (Collins 1999: 78; Collins and Davis 2004: 78). How the film reverberates – sometimes ambitiously, sometimes uncomfortably, somewhat incompletely – with such events forms a central part of the discussion of the film later in the chapter.

Towards the end of the 1970s, the number of period movies produced in Australia began to taper off.[4] AFC funding policies, on which period movies depended, were supplanted by the 10BA policy, which encouraged different forms of filmmaking. Graeme Turner and others have argued that audiences were ready to turn away from a genre that was essentially conservative and that the genre's characters ceased to be suitable for a nation that was in search of more relevant, contemporary stories (Turner 1989: 115; Ryan 1980; Moran and Vieth 2006; Cunningham 2009). In Tom Ryan's words, typical period film subjects were victims of history, not its agents (Ryan, quoted in Turner 1989: 115).

As I will go on to show, these words could not be less applicable to the lead female protagonists in Armstrong's two Australian-set period films. They are nonetheless tonally consistent with the derogatory responses of some critics who appear to have been unable to look past the genre's perceived feminine themes and projected female audiences. Keith Connolly's (1981) sexist denigration of the 'lacy Victorian frocks' in *Picnic at Hanging Rock* would comprise an example of this, as would Jay Scott's quip that *Picnic* was 'beautiful' yet 'coy' and said to possess a 'pulp sensibility'; Scott went on to say that viewing the movie was akin to 'esthetic coitus interruptus' (Scott 1979). Produced towards the very end of the Australian period film cycle of the 1970s, *My Brilliant Career* did not completely escape this kind of commentary; one critic, Adele Freedman, for example called Judy Davis's character a girl 'who can't say yes' (Freedman 1980).[5]

While current-day valuations of period movies do not always contain the blatant sexism evident in late seventies/early eighties evaluations, period films continue to be devalued or at least overlooked in the assessments of some current-day critics, who retroactively applaud Australian generic innovations but now no longer see period films as a genre. For example, Mark Ryan's iteration of the history of Australian genre filmmaking includes 'action-adventure, science fiction, comedy, crime, romance, suspense thriller, musicals and horror movies' (2012: 142); the timeline Ryan gives for these iterations includes movies produced from 1970 to 1975, from 1981 to 1988, and from 2007 to 2008 (144–5). In this reckoning, the years between 1975 and 1981 when *My Brilliant Career* was produced are a genre-free space.

By and large, in spite of these taxonomical oversights and interpretive slights, Armstrong's work has risen above most negative perceptions of the genre. *My Brilliant Career* particularly has been singled out as an exception to what has been assessed as a conventional form (Moran and Vieth 2006: 37) and critical regard for it appears to have grown over time. This is evidenced by the 2018 selection of the film to be digitised, restored, and preserved for the purpose of ensuring that Australian audiences could enjoy 'culturally significant films' and/or 'popular films that have resonated with the media and the public'.[6]

My Brilliant Career

My Brilliant Career is an adaptation of the Federation-era coming-of-age novel by Miles Franklin (1901) about a young woman who aspires to be a writer in rural New South Wales. The novel makes use of the first-person point of view of Sybylla Melvyn and has been interpreted as a '"passionate protest and revolt of a gifted, untutored girl against the deadening slavery" of the lives of wives of small farmers' (Magarey 2002: 396).[7] In addition to being in sympathy with first-wave feminism, the book's entwinement with discourses of nation-invention has been noted (Devlin-Glass 2011); this is evident in Sybylla's concluding declaration, 'I am proud that I am an Australian, a daughter of the Southern Cross, a child of the mighty bush' (Franklin 1980: 231). Like other expressions of nationalism at this time, Sybylla's national affections are often pro-working class (Devlin-Glass 2011: 83). The novel shows sympathy for those who work for a living and/or live in poverty, indicated by Sybylla's comment that 'In poverty, you can get at the real heart of people as you can never do if rich. People are your friends from pure friendship and love, not from sponging self-interestedness' (Franklin 1980: 24). However the class aspects of the novel are not at all straightforward; while the family falls on hard times when the father moves them from the genteel environs of Caddagat to the remote cattle station in

Possum Gully and becomes a 'slave of drink' (Franklin 1980: 14), Sybylla's mother begins life as a 'full-fledged aristocrat' (Franklin 1980: 2) and much of Sybylla's time in the novel is spent aspirationally hoping for a secure and permanent position at her grandmother's estate.

Making use of a screenplay by Eleanor Witcombe, the film retains the novel's point of view and most of its major events. Armstrong was approached to direct the movie by producer Margaret Fink who had seen and been impressed by Armstrong's 1930s-set period short, *One Hundred a Day*. Like the novel, the film centres the story around the charismatic and independently minded young female protagonist. Like the novel, the film acknowledges the advantages of upper-class life but is told from the perspective of someone whose class position is insecure. Like the novel, the film takes place across a spectrum of iconic Australian landscapes; these include the drought-affected Possum Gully, the lush gardens surrounding Sybylla's grandmother's Caddagat home, and the expansive green lawns around Five-Bob Downs. Memorable sequences depict post and rail fences with a still river in the background, a dam encircled by gum trees, a pen brimming with sheep waiting to be shorn, and interiors of various stately Victorian homes. Cinematography by Don McAlpine captures a range of lighting conditions, from sun-bleached landscapes to the blue-grey twilight forest of Australian ferns which Harry and Sybylla ride through en route to Five-Bob Downs. As in the novel, Sybylla's career aspirations end up trumping her romantic desires, as she rejects the marriage proposal that comes at the movie's end from her better-resourced suitor, Harry Beecham (played by Sam Neill) – an event that seemed as cinematically surprising in 1979 as it was socially taboo in 1901.

The establishing shot of *My Brilliant Career* shows a farmhouse set in the distance in a wide field of tawny-coloured grass, as Judy Davis's voice-over identifies the story time and place: Possum Gully, Australia, 1897. The subsequent shot focuses on the house and front veranda as Judy Davis steps into the frame. Davis is positioned inside the house, reading aloud from a paper notebook: 'Dear fellow countrymen, just a few lines to let you know that this story is going to be all about me.' As if both to pose and answer her own question, Davis lowers the script, takes a breath, and continues: 'Here is the story of my career. Here is the story of my career? My *brilliant* career.' From this point the scene cross cuts between Davis reading from her developing autobiography and two men who struggle to muster cattle outside in the glaring, sun-drenched, bone-dry foreground. Outdoors the dust storm clouds visibility and the howling wind and lowing cattle make Davis's voice nearly inaudible. Separated from the howling wind, lowing cattle, and mid-ground nearly whited-out from dust, Sybylla Melvyn sits behind the glass window and clarifies that she makes 'no apology for being egotistical because I am. I have always known that I belonged to the world of art and the world of literature and music.'

To audiences not yet exposed to the brash, exhibitionist performances of post-feminist pop-culture heroines which would circulate globally in less than ten years, Judy Davis's confident and iconoclastic yet searching character would have been humorous and enjoyable; for cinema-goers perhaps more accustomed to American icons than Australian stars, the complex young woman protagonist would have seemed nothing short of revolutionary. Evaluations of Armstrong's career leave no doubt about the role played by *My Brilliant Career* in the director's professional life. Directing the movie put Armstrong on the global stage and provided her, Davis, and Fink with the invaluable opportunity to represent Australia at Cannes when the movie was put in competition in 1979.[8] Interviews with the three of them from the festival were broadcast to a national audience on Australian television. In addition to Cannes, the film was shown at the New York film festival, won six Australian Film Institute awards, and a BAFTA for Davis as best actress in a leading role.

Although the coming-of-age story had been seen in Australian films prior to *My Brilliant Career*, the film broke ground in developing the coming-of-age story into a claim for an adult woman's independence. Other Australian films had targeted female audiences and featured female protagonists, but the most successful had focused on school*girls* (*Picnic at Hanging Rock* (Peter Weir, 1975) and *The Getting of Wisdom* (Bruce Beresford, 1977)). The film was ahead of its time in making the connection between women's independence and literary authorship and in centring the story around a woman artist. The international arthouse cycle of artist-centred, woman-oriented biopics about Sylvia Plath (2003), Jane Austen (2007), Janet Frame (1990), Virginia Woolf (2002), and Iris Murdoch (2001) was still fifteen years away.

The value of women authors to serve as textual markers of women's agency more broadly has been pointed out by Shelley Cobb, who writes that Armstrong's film is the 'foremother' of films about women writers because of how it 'grants discursive authority to a collective female voice outside the texts ... [and aligns] this voice with a female figure within the text' (Thornham 2012: 93; quoted in Cobb 2015: 15). Cobb identifies the multiple ways women may establish authority within film; these include working as film director, script writer, and serving as depicted author of the subject material.

Sybylla's authority is depicted within the very first few shots of the film, when she confidently utters the word 'brilliant' in reference to her own career. At this moment, *My Brilliant Career* immediately and unabashedly fuses character and quality together and confirms the character's agentic power to be responsible for her own self-authoring. In doing this, the film surpasses the intentions of the novel where the word 'brilliant' does not appear until page 33, and then in reference to Sybylla's looks (Franklin 1980: 57). In this way *My Brilliant Career* gives rise to a complex, empowered, and charismatic female character suited to the contemporary moment.

In addition to brilliance, Davis's character is associated with qualities of defiance, independence, and uniqueness, through formidable exclamations like 'God be damned!' and wordless, bodily actions, such as her slamming down the piano lid when interrupted by her mother, stomping away from the milking cows, and capable wielding of a wood axe. In the early Possum Gully sequence, these appear (largely) as evidence of teenage rebellion, but subsequent scenes after she arrives at her grandmother's home code such actions as expressions of individualistic exuberance of a young adult woman. What sets the film apart from Franklin's book, perhaps through the power and strength of Judy Davis's performance, is its delineation of Sybylla as a mercurial character, capable of exuding adolescent petulance, class apprehension, depth of character, and liberal feminist power, within a matter of moments. The extended close-up on Davis's face and hands when she is seated at a formal dinner in her grandmother's house as she spoons food on to her plate with trepidation and meticulous care, captures her understanding of her place towards the bottom of the class hierarchy and concern not to make a social blunder. The look on her face conveys her knowledge of her own precarity as a guest in the home, and otherness hailing from the remote outback.

Elsewhere the film delights in sending up those with upper-class pretentions, and other scenes indicate Sybylla's dextrous ability to correctly interpret and sometimes subvert class rules. For example, Sybylla's adoption of a 'cockney' 'maid's' accent when first encountering Harry Beecham both draws attention to Harry's own inability to understand female and/or class stereotypes and Sybylla's multilingual competence as a code-switcher comfortable in all social/class registers. In the scene, Harry encounters Sybylla high up in a tree and interprets the sight of her petticoats as evidence of her sexual availability and (he believes) working-class status. Grasping his error, Sybylla playfully adopts the fake accent and makes no effort to correct him. When later they meet at the family party, Harry is appalled when he realises his mistake. Though the scene is consistent with what is in Franklin's book, the lingering shot showing Harry's stricken face further emphasises the depth of the mistake.

As has been described at the outset of this section, Franklin's novel contains strong elements of class critique and nationalism moulded with first-wave feminist sentiment; the film largely builds on and augments these elements. For example, when aristocrat Frank Hawdon expresses his entitled assumption that Sybylla will marry and return to England with him – which scene appears in the novel and which offer Sybylla roundly rejects – the two-shot in the film is followed by a comedic shot of Frank toppling over backwards into a sheep pen, which does not appear in the Franklin iteration. While novel-Sybylla relates the story of Aunt Helen's desertion by her husband (Franklin 1980: 48), in the film Aunt Helen takes initiative to tell this story herself: 'My husband isn't dead', she says to Sybylla in an intimate two-shot, 'he left me for someone else. He left me to live the rest of my life with the shame of being neither wife, nor widow, nor maid.' While the film does not alter the facts of Aunt Helen's life, it grants new agency in allowing her to tell it. The film rendition, I believe, attributes a subtle but powerful authoring agency to the wronged woman in the story, which is absent from the novel's first-person telling.

Through such subtle changes in narration and *mise-en-scène* and, as stated above, the power of Davis's performance, Armstrong rallies the potency of cinema to augment and update the novel's original feminist and class politics for 1970s consumption. The concluding sequences of the story are worth considering in detail. Towards the end of both the film and novel, Harry proposes to Sybylla one last time. In the novel, Sybylla's negative response is issued via a note which she slips into his hand; in the film, Judy Davis turns to Sam Neill and delivers an impassioned feminist utterance: 'The last thing I want is to be a wife out in the bush, having a baby every year.' Davis then clarifies her staunch desire to become a writer, which must be done 'now' and 'alone'. As elsewhere in the movie, the Australian landscape lingers in audiences' memories, as the final shot of the sequence situates the couple in the midst of a dusty, pale-brown-coloured, flat expanse, punctuated by remnants of a few dead trees. The following scene, of Davis alone, recalls and bookends the movie's opening scene. It shows Sybylla finishing her novel at her desk while her voice-over describes her affection for her country: 'How I love them [my people] and pity them. Pity all of us. The sun is shining another day, and hope is whispering in my ear. With love and good wishes to all. Good night. Good bye. Amen.' While these words are quite close to what Franklin wrote, what is different is the film's closing words, that are not in the novel. In the film, Sybylla continues:

> So now I've written it all down. Why? To try and make sense of it. It may come out sounding like a couple of nails in a rusty tin pot. My ineffectual life may be trod in the same round of toil. But I want to tell everyone about my own people.

In this final self-reflexive coda, which does not appear in Franklin's book, the film accomplishes a number of things: it references Sybylla's status as a writer and author of the remarks, confers voice and agency on her, and emphasises her authorial power. *My Brilliant Career* thus anticipates the many films, mentioned above, that centre on women writers' lives and the many movies that Armstrong will go on to make that give voice to disempowered and female protagonists. Secondly, the prominent inclusion of the phrase 'my people' at the very end of the utterance confirms the film's aspirations around the project of nation-building, and in so doing fuses protagonist and filmmaker ambitions to tell not only gendered stories but ones with national relevance. In doing this, the final coda underscores and highlights the unique joining of feminist, class, and nationalist concerns.

The closing scene revisits the film's opening scene, but now placing Sybylla firmly in control. Sybylla is again shown reading aloud indoors, but unlike the first scene, is shown venturing outside and placing the now finished manuscript in the post box, to go off to the publisher. As the theme music swells, Sybylla hangs off the wide farm gate, her golden, radiant face shown smiling with the sun fully on it, as the sun sets in the distance. The colours resemble those used in the opening but now seen through the prism of Sybylla's achievements, the harsh country of the opening scene is re-rendered to become extraordinary and sublime. The result is a recuperation of the Australian landscape, as enjoyed by an Anglo-Australian woman protagonist, a confirmation of the place of that protagonist within the Australian period film cycle, and a confirmation of themes identified in this book's introduction, such as the importance of women's journeys, and women's independence from men.

Oscar and Lucinda

Armstrong's second Australian-set period film *Oscar and Lucinda* (1997) shares with *My Brilliant Career* a number of important components; these include the nineteenth-century Australian setting, the engagement with themes of history and place, a script drawn from a well-regarded Australian novel, Peter Carey's 1988 *Oscar and Lucinda*, and the featuring of an iconoclastic and independently minded Anglo-Australian female protagonist. Like *My Brilliant Career*, *Oscar and Lucinda* depicts the stranglehold of social and religious mores, which the lead woman character is uniquely able to critique: as Sybylla in *My Brilliant Career* enjoyed teasing the aristocratic Harry, Lucinda in the later film likewise appears to take pleasure in scandalising middle-brow Sydney society. In a departure from *My Brilliant Career*, *Oscar and Lucinda* weaves its story around – not one, but – two main characters, whose cross-class romance extends and to a certain extent complicates the nationalist colonial imaginary of the earlier movie. And where *My Brilliant Career*'s Australia was largely racially homogeneous, the later film offers an emergent multiculturalism in its vision of urban Sydney and an image of the Australian bush that is populated by Indigenous citizens. As I will go on to discuss, *Oscar and Lucinda*'s figuring of racialised history is complex and ambitious but not unproblematic.

Lucinda Leplastrier (Cate Blanchett) is an Australian heiress and entrepreneur who uses her inheritance to purchase a glass factory in Sydney. Oscar Hopkins (Ralph Fiennes) is the repressed son of a Plymouth Brethren preacher who renounces his faith and migrates from England to the new colony as self-inflicted punishment for his inability to stop gambling. Oscar and Lucinda discover their shared obsession with betting on the Sydney-bound ship. After arriving, the relationship blossoms into an undeclared yet passionate *folie à deux*-styled romance, fuelled by their mutual obsession. Too repressed to openly declare his love, Oscar offers to lead a difficult expedition transporting a glass church overland, in hopes that the gesture will express what he cannot say in words. Together Oscar and Lucinda appoint a technically capable foreman, Jeffris: more straightfor- wardly ruthless than in Carey's novel, Jeffris is the film's unique articulation of white settler racism in his disdain for Indigenous Australians and their sovereign ownership of country. Where Carey's novel contains evidence of casual racism voiced by several characters, Armstrong's film condenses these aspects on to this single character. When the church comes to be transported, the film implies challenges in negotiating passage with the Aboriginal owners; Jeffris's 'solution' is to seek out a tribe of Kumbaingiri men and boys and shoot all of them in cold blood. Oscar then takes an axe to Jeffris and kills him; this and the terrible events of the massacre leave him so distraught that at the journey's end he becomes the victim of a terrible accident and drowns.

Released eighteen years after *My Brilliant Career* and on the heels of several American studio successes and numerous feted Australian films, *Oscar and Lucinda* occupies a very different space than *My Brilliant Career* both on Armstrong's CV and with respect to contemporary Australian history. By the time *Oscar and Lucinda* was released in the late 1990s the second-wave-inflected feminist concerns of the 1970s may not have seemed quite so pressing, allowing the 1997 film to hew more closely to the generic features of a romance. It accomplishes this by placing new star Cate Blanchett (in her first leading role) and Oscar-nominated Fiennes on screen together for more time than what occurs in Carey's novel (Armstrong brings the characters together in the first third of the movie, where in Carey's novel Oscar and Lucinda do not actually meet until the second half of the book).

In addition to bringing forward the time frame of the cha- racters' meeting, cinematography and editing connote the strength and significance of Oscar and Lucinda's relationship. At one moment, Lucinda's abrupt departure from her business partner's rooms is followed by a tracking shot of a dog fight; audiences expect to see Lucinda's face but instead Oscar's comes into view. On the ship, a shot tracks from four deckhands playing cards to a metal grate behind which audiences assume they will spy Oscar's face; the next shot shows Lucinda's. The cinematography, by Geoffrey Simpson, and joining together of these scenes contribute to audiences' sense of the inevitability of the romance and position gambling as the relationship emollient.

Perhaps more than any other of Armstrong's movies, *Oscar and Lucinda* develops the two characters' backstories in perfect congruence; this approach also contrasts somewhat with Carey's version of events, where Lucinda does not appear until after the first seventy pages, when Oscar renounces his father's religion. In Armstrong's version, Lucinda is actually introduced prior to Oscar: shots show the title 'New South Wales 1848' and a close-up on a little girl's face with adult hands covering the eyes, as adults cry 'Surprise!' It is Lucinda's birthday and the surprise is a glass trinket (a Prince Rupert's drop). Directly following this scene, the title 'Devon England' appears and we see little boy Oscar running to the water's edge, following his father who throws his dead wife's clothes into the sea. 'Christmas day 8 years later' shows teenage Oscar surreptitiously tasting a delicious, forbidden pudding, with his father knocking it from his mouth with a forceful swat; a shot of Lucinda swimming in a waterhole follows directly after. Parallel cross-cutting such as this emphasises the profoundly different religious, class, and cultural backgrounds Lucinda and Oscar come from and the poignancy of the romance. In a revival of pro-nationalist themes seen in *My Brilliant Career*, cross-cutting also positions turn of the century Sydney as the progressive locale, offering the freedom necessary for the unlikely romance to flourish.

In keeping with the nationalist strains of Australian period cinema, the Australian (Lucinda) and the Englishman (Oscar) bring quite different skill sets to negotiate the Sydney metropolis.

For Oscar, careening overhead shots of dense greenery and the loud sound of insects suggest disorientation, in contrast to Lucinda's experience, for whom developing Sydney provides opportunities for well-to-do Anglo-Australian women to conduct business and even cohabit with other white men with only relatively minor negative consequences. As in both *My Brilliant Career* and Carey's novel, there are scenes asserting women's entitlement to the public sphere and men's ignorance about these matters, as when Hasset, the man who will become Lucinda's business partner, expects a *Monsieur* Leplastrier and a *Madame* arrives instead.

The presence of the present

Where the rural spaces in *My Brilliant Career* were physically harsh but ultimately able to be tamed by white landowners, *Oscar and Lucinda* corrects the mistaken idea that the Australian bush is 'freely' available for un-negotiated traversals by white settler Australians. In the post-Mabo period, white presumption of ownership of country must be challenged. Inside this new imagining, the 'overland' can no longer be unproblematically converted into an object of white nostalgia because the colonial-era presumption of 'free' passage (progressing to white ownership) is no longer tenable; the overland is construed as danger-filled instead.

Once the expedition gets underway, tense music accompanies extreme long shots of the dramatic and steep terrain. Wagons become stuck in the mud; the white explorers/invaders are completely out of their depth. While Carey's novel has Oscar tied up by Jeffris's men prior to the attack on the Aboriginal men, in Armstrong's version, Oscar jettisons himself forward into the scene, as Jeffris shoots. Oscar is dragged away and there is an overhead shot of two young Aboriginal men, with blood-spattered torsos, one with an arm casually draped over other; the shot is held for a full fifteen seconds, while the dying man's body shakes and gurgling is heard. This is the most graphic shot in the film and possibly the most graphic shot across the whole of Armstrong's career; the camera holds for what seems a very long time on their suffering bodies. Directly after the massacre, extreme long shots show the caravan making its way down from the pass, accompanied again by foreboding music. Oscar takes a swig of laudanum, while Jeffris – the movie's unreconstructed representative of pre-Mabo racism – is emboldened by what he has just done and asks, 'How goes life in the ladies' compartment?' And, with an evil smile deriving from his erroneous misapprehension of his ownership, 'What d'ya say to this countryside?'

More than any others in her entire body of work, these scenes confirm Armstrong's engagement with a politics of Indigenous sovereignty and an empathy born of post-Mabo understanding. In other scenes of the film, in other locations, the politics are more murky. The demography of urban Sydney conforms, as said, to a limited form of multiculturalism, via the Chinese underclass who populate and control the shadowy gambling underworld in what now seems a somewhat stereotypical way. And conspicuously, the city does not appear to include a single Indigenous inhabitant. This appears a departure from both the novel (which refers on occasion to Indigenous Sydney-dwellers) and the historical record, where an Aboriginal presence in greater Sydney in the mid-nineteenth century has been documented (Ireland 2013; Karskens 2009; Kavenagh 2009; Goodall and Cadzow 2009; Osmond 2017). Although fictional films are clearly not required to be historically faithful, the decision to create a cityscape devoid of an Indigenous presence has consequences for the post-Mabo vision that the film ultimately is able to offer. In contrast to the Australian bush, the metropolis fantasised by the film appears unaffected by – cordoned off from – the Mabo findings; it can thus still function as symbol of pre-Mabo, white Australian identity and a holdout against revisionist understandings of place that the Mabo case precipitated.

In their writing about post-Mabo Australian cinema, Collins and Davis delineate the capacity for landscape cinema (of which

Oscar and Lucinda is an example) to produce symptoms of 'aftershock', that is, unpredictable, multi-impactful events or processes which foster new recognitions of history's impact on current-day circumstances. Collins and Davis associate Armstrong's film with the

> familiar shock of recognition, of being shocked again, of becoming unshockable as more and more landscape images after Mabo evoke a traumatic colonial history ... Our use of the term to describe post-Mabo cinema implies that Indigenous and settler Australians alike are still living through the unresolved trauma of colonial settlement. (2004: 81)

It would seem that this 'unresolvedness' is unequally meted out. In the discussion at the start of this section I indicated how Armstrong's film shifts Carey's story to more fully encompass Lucinda's side of the events; in keeping with Armstrong's stated interest in telling women's stories, the ending of the movie departs from Carey's book in similar ways. Where the book concludes with the moment of Oscar's death, the film's final shots depict several events after this: Lucinda visiting the place where Oscar died, her several-years-later cavorting with Oscar's child in the water, and a shot of Oscar's great-grandson (the story's narrator) motoring away from the camera in a small boat with a girl we presume is his daughter. It should be clarified that none of these ending images feature in the book.

For a film that would seem otherwise to be interested in amplifying and extending the original story parameters to explore possibilities for female agency and women's physical traversals of the cityscape, it is a disappointment that white women's involvement with Indigeneity and colonialism remains unexplored. Confined largely to a city populated exclusively by white and Chinese people, Lucinda's engagement with Indigenous Australians remains unfigured. The contest over passage through, and entitlement to, the overland is a thoroughly masculine one; women's participations in such events are not spelled out. Though

Aboriginal women do figure in the story – both Carey's and Armstrong's depictions show the rape of an Aboriginal woman by a member of the expedition – white women remained confined to the (white/Chinese) urban centre and thus at a distance from the genocidal apparatuses of settler state colonialism. Just as Lucinda at the movie's beginning is prevented from seeing (when her eyes are covered on her birthday), she likewise does not view the colonial massacre that Oscar has no choice but to witness and participate in. And thus she remains ignorant to the catastrophe, just as audience members remain ignorant to the historical role played by white women in the settlement/invasion activities of the white colonists.

In *The Cultural Politics of Emotion* (2014), Sara Ahmed asks what it means to craft an identity through the practice of shame, and posits the potential role shame may serve in projects of nation-building such as in Australia in the wake of the release of the Bringing Them Home report (102). In Ahmed's formulation, shame is not a moment in a move to pride, but a crucial first step after sorry (120). Important for the context of *Oscar and Lucinda*, shame requires a witness to 'catch out' the 'failure of the individual to live up to an ego ideal' (108).

It is not difficult to see in the character of Oscar the embodiment of the emotions and affects Ahmed delineates. Oscar is witness to Jeffris's murdering of the Indigenous men and the living embodiment of shame in the story. After Jeffris commits the murders and Oscar responds violently and kills him with an axe, he becomes nearly catatonic. Shortly after the journey ends, Oscar falls asleep from the exhaustion of the recent experiences, inside the glass church he has promised to transport for Lucinda, as it slides into the river. Ironically trapped inside the crowning physical achievement of the colonial missionary project, Oscar drowns.

Felicity Collins has claimed that Armstrong's period movies are characterised by freedom from nostalgia (1999: 78). Indeed, there is no nostalgia in either *Brilliant Career*'s or *Oscar and Lucinda*'s telling of Australian history or in the positioning of white women (in the case of *Brilliant Career*), or missionaries or

Indigenous men (in the case of *Oscar and Lucinda*) within those stories. The respective historical narratives that are on offer are complexly contoured with negative emotions of suffering, loss, and (in the case of *Oscar and Lucinda* in particular), shame. While the two films end on nominally happy notes – Sybylla sends off her manuscript, as described, and Lucinda is seen playing with Oscar's child – in both cases the happy affect is tempered by knowledge of depicted and contemporary events of women's disenfranchisement (in *Brilliant Career*) and colonial genocide (in *Oscar and Lucinda*). Oscar's premature death following the expedition leaves Lucinda to raise his child on her own, while Sybylla is required to relinquish claims to her male partner. In both cases, history is consequential and, to invoke Fredric Jameson, what hurts (1982).

While Armstrong's Australian period films were made within historical contexts which I have delineated, there is evidence that the genre remains perhaps even more relevant in the post-2000 period and able to touch on a spectrum of current concerns such as mental illness, sexual assault, and Indigenous sovereignty. In the post-2000s, period films remain popular, socioculturally significant forms with expressly gendered appeal. *Rabbit-Proof Fence* (2002) and *The Dressmaker* (2015) are two critically acclaimed iterations which were popular with audiences and which put women at the centre of their stories; Jennifer Kent's 'necessarily brutal' *The Nightingale* (2018) – labelled a 'song of violence and vengeance' and a 'labour of rage' – is the most recognised recent expression (Behrendt 2018; Scott 2019; O'Malley 2019).

The Australian musical: *Starstruck*

In the longer view of Australian cinema history, musicals comprise some of the most beloved Australian-set films and some of the most financially successful internationalised films helmed by Australian directors. *Moulin Rouge!* (2001), directed by Baz Lurhmann, is rated the sixth top-grossing Australian film of all time,[9] with *The Adventures of Priscilla, Queen of the Desert* (1994) also bringing in profit well above its production costs.[10] Musicals have long caught the attention of queer studies scholars, and their provision of opportunities for the expression of non-hegemonic masculinities and performative gender identity has been recognised. As David Gerstner puts it 'to write about the film musical as an *objet de queer* is, in short, redundant' (2010: 188).

Many of the most beloved and well-known Australian musicals explicitly feature gender and/or racially diverse characters and join musical expression with expressions of gendered and raced identities. It has been written that Priscilla 'defined a decade of Australian cinema and truly opened up the filmic reservoirs for more mainstream and positive representations of diverse LGBT folks on screen' as well as spawning a highly successful Broadway revival (Smith 2014). *The Sapphires, Bran Nue Day* (2009) and the non-feature musical *One Night the Moon* (2001) each centre their stories around Indigenous characters and were helmed by Indigenous-majority production teams. With its incorporation of African American music and setting in the time and place of the Vietnam war, *The Sapphires* refurbishes an American expression that, according to Desirée J. Garcia (2014), has depended on rhetorics from Black-cast musicals since at least the 1920s. As with the two Australian-set period movies, the movies succeed in inserting Australian features (characters, iconography, and landscapes) into hegemonic forms and providing a cinematic space where emotion can be expressed.

Gillian Armstrong's *Starstruck* is a youth-oriented musical feature that tracks the rags-to-riches story of New-Wave-styled singer Jackie Mullins and her 14-year-old cousin and band manager, Angus. Released only four years after the very first Sydney Lesbian and Gay Mardi Gras, *Starstruck* seems from a current day, post-queer theory perspective, hugely ahead of its time in the vibrant alternatives to gender- and heteronormativity which it depicts and in its joyous exploration of identity and performance. While *Starstruck's* two lead characters are nominally cast as heterosexual, the film delights in interrupting gender norms at every turn: screen time is given to non-mainstream pairings, like Jackie and the gay musical producer Terry. Angus's masculinity appears purely performative, a show put on to impress (his first object of desire is a mannequin he sees in a shop window). High camp, male-led musical numbers feature handsome lifeguards and other toy boys in fantasy sequences which are wholly disconnected from the story. Throughout, Jackie is decked out in bright, mismatched fabrics with spunky teased-up red hair, while Angus sports bright blue hair and a full-size kangaroo outfit. Jackie's and Angus's lives are dedicated wholly to 'making it' in the music industry and no stunt is too outrageous, including Jackie's dangling from a tightrope above the Sydney streets wearing fake breasts with leather regalia.

Armstrong's attachment to *Starstruck* arose from a strong desire on her part to depart from the genre of movies set in the past about women achievers with which (after *Brilliant Career*) she had become identified. Making the movie capitalised on the director's self-proclaimed interest in the-atricality and performance, and in hindsight its musical and comedic components frame it as a kind of queer interruption of Armstrong's professional trajectory and exploration into a genre to which she would never again return.[11]

Shot in and around well-known landmarks of Sydney with new performers Jo Kennedy and Ross O'Donovan and musical contribution from the New Zealand band The Swingers, Armstrong's second feature charts Jackie's rise from hotel barmaid to Sydney Opera House performing sensation. The two cousins live above the Harbour View Hotel with their family, who comprise a colourful cast of eccentrics which include Jackie's mother Pearl, the cockatoo-bedecked Uncle Reg, and Jackie and Angus's nana. While Pearl and other family members initially tut-tut Jackie's ambitions and criticise the time Angus spends out of school, by the end of the movie they are won over when Jackie's Opera House performance earns prize money that will go towards saving the financially stressed pub.

With its emphasis on themes of performance and show business, *Starstruck* is a prime example of the backstage musical: movies that centre the story around the challenges and pleasures of people 'getting together and putting on a show' (Feuer 2012: 543). Backstage musicals often focus on the day-to-day workings of the entertainment industry and demonstrate the 'mythification' of entertainment as an effect of spontaneity and integration. They perpetuate the idea that the industry is a meritocratic system where hard work pays off in the end (Feuer 2012: 544–5). Further themes of the backstage musical include audience participation and the importance of family, from which performers often need to break free.

In *Starstruck*, musical scenes set before 'live' audiences convey the impression of spontaneity, with many numbers featuring singing and dancing by members of the audience. In the lead-up to Jackie's big break, initial rifts with band members and family bubble up but ultimately are smoothed over. Jackie's attempt to succeed on her own is revealed to be misguided and her final triumph the result of the reunion of Jackie with the original band. Individual eccentricities are encouraged, most obviously in Jackie and Angus, but also in Nana who breaks away from the pub to pursue life as a clairvoyant. Aspiration is underwritten by an ideology of egalitarian meritocracy and domestic success is closely entwined with professional success. As Angus relays the game plan to Jackie: 'We rehearse the band, we find an image, we crack the opera house, then we save the pub!' And indeed, as the final scene cuts back and forth between Jackie and the band's triumph at the Opera House and the family celebrating back home in the pub, this appears to have come true.

In addition to the messages of fair work, happiness, and community that it promulgates, *Starstruck* incorporates qualities of self-reflexivity, including issues of fame, stardom, and performance that reflect on their own conditions of possibility. Set in the world of show business, backstage musicals justify, via their narratives, opportunities for performers to 'burst' into song and dance, in spontaneous-appearing albeit highly choreographed ways. Via their narrative inclusion of scenes such as rehearsals, auditions, and the build-up to the big performance, these musicals fold opportunities for singing and dancing into their storylines. Backstage musicals thus both comprise entertainment in their own right and may serve as localised meta-commentaries on the business of entertainment, with respect to the time and context in question.

In Feuer's historical reckoning, backstage musicals became especially important in the 1950s, at a time when movie studios could no longer assume audience allegiance. In Feuer's contextualised reading, musicals such as *Singin' in the Rain* could provide solutions in times of social and technological change and foster self-serving myths to generate 'buzz' and interest through their very storylines. In spite of its production thirty years after the time Feuer addresses and half a world away, *Starstruck* was produced in a moment of dramatic policy shift in Australian film funding, which saw the winding up of government grants that had underwritten many productions through the 1970s (including many extended to period movies) and ushering in the more overtly commercial risk-encouraging 10BA scheme. Frequently generous in the economic returns that it guaranteed and often associated with a more overtly commercial outlook, the 10BA has been associated with movies like *Mad Max*, which was hugely popular but whose relation to a national agenda was unclear. As Ian Craven has written, 'The 1980s has been characterised as an era of de-regulation, encroachment by the market, and a new commercialism aesthetics' (Craven 2001: 2; quoted in Ryan and Goldsmith 2017: 1). Not a moment of *technological* change as identified by Feuer, *Starstruck* must be read in relation to these *policy* changes, which its themes of meritocratic performance and entertainment positivity could not but help mitigate.

In light of such policy shifts, *Starstruck*'s setting in the Australian context and flagging of apparently Australian attributes is all the more notable. Jackie and Angus are fans of American pop culture but posters of Lauren Bacall and Elvis

Presley which they display in their home are frequently overshadowed by more localised icons and images. The film is shot in and around Sydney, including the tightrope scene, with iconic edifices such as the Opera House and the Sydney Harbour Bridge featuring as backdrop (Collins 1999: 33). In the Harbour View hotel, which is a real Sydney pub, a giant image of the Sydney Harbour Bridge is part of the decor. Dance sequences like Jackie's surfboard performance (where the ironing board doubles as a surfboard) play tribute to and poke fun at so-termed Australian holiday elements, beach and sun, while Australian and Australian-associated animals (cockatoos, kangaroos, sharks) pepper the *mise-en-scène*. The movie featured one song which became a hit single on the Australian charts, 'She Got Body She Got Soul', penned by Tim Finn of the Australian band *Split Enz*. The film's dizzying, celebratory conclusion takes place within the Opera House itself, assisted by scores of un-professional schoolchildren serving as audience, and brought into relief the film's unique combining of icons of high and low cultures with its focus on youth cultures.

To sum up, with its mythification of the labour of musical performance, last-minute solving of the family's entrenched financial woes, and feel-good, happy ending that sees all characters harmoniously reunited, *Starstruck* must not be mistaken for critical political commentary. But this is not the point of backstage musical genre movies; instead, *Starstruck* displays Armstrong's deft command of a genre with which she had little prior experience and ability to create a vibrant, pro-queer, pro-youth, Australian-centred work, in part by means of a rough aesthetic that marked a clear departure from the AFC-financed films of the prior decade. Armstrong's prescience in bringing all these concerns together within the single film is echoed in the stated theme of the 1981 Sydney Lesbian and Gay Mardi Gras (by then only in its fourth year, as stated) 'We are the People our Parents Warned us Against'. Released less than one year later, *Starstruck* identified, brought together, and further provided voice for these ideals and concerns.

Conclusion

Deborah Jermyn has written compellingly about the critical resistance to take seriously women creators of genre movies (2018). While popular movies may be a potent means for the incorporation of political and sometimes controversial themes about class, sexuality, and/or race, Jermyn notes the critical bias against such forms and unwillingness to recognise women filmmakers working in these spaces. Of Nancy Meyers, Jermyn writes:

> [B]ut what is striking and significant in the reception of Meyers is how much more tremendously vocal the critical voices pointing to conservative readings of her films have been to date, so that attention has barely been paid to any potential to locate other, more textured, inharmonious or even reformist commentary at work in her oeuvre. There is an outright resistance to the possibility she could have anything more than one-dimensional vision – a resistance that pivots on the generic substance of her films, their industrial genesis in Hollywood and the fact of her gender. And it is in part this troubling matrix that future work on Meyers needs to examine as it goes forward, if she is not to become another half-remembered woman only discontinuously glimpsed on the edges of film history. (Jermyn 2018: 70)

Audiences of popular commercial genre movies are obviously not hapless dupes. This chapter has examined how Armstrong's Australian-shot films rework international genre settings, iconography, and other attributes for a local context. The chapter has demonstrated the wide reach of Armstrong's achievements. The chapter has considered how Armstrong has adapted and utilised popular generic forms (the period film and the backstage musical) with multiple effects. The chapter has canvassed the films' incorporation of generic themes and characters into Australian settings and production contexts to transform them in unique and new ways.

Notes

1 But importantly, *not* from the Australian Film Commission (AFC) Project funding, and with corporate support from Greater Union Organisation.
2 *Starstruck* received support from the AFC. Available at <https://pro.imdb.com/title/tt0084728/companycredits> (last accessed 13 April 2020).
3 The connection was so close that Australian period films were named the AFC genre (Dermody and Jacka 1988: 31–7).
4 In fact, *My Brilliant Career* struggled to gain funding on account of the perception that there was a glut of such movies; it was finally co-produced by the New South Wales Film Commission and Greater Union (*not* the AFC).
5 Period films were called 'worthy but dull' and *Brilliant Career* was famously called 'taxidermy' by Pauline Kael (Turner 1989: 100).
6 The film was selected into the programme NFSA Restores. Available at <https://www.nfsa.gov.au/about/our-mission/nfsa-restores> (last accessed 13 April 2020).
7 Magarey is quoting 10 February 1902, p. 142. *Australian Women's Sphere*, East Melbourne, VIC. Printed and published by Vida Goldstein, 1900–5.
8 It is well known that shortly after this success, the director soon found herself inundated with scripts, many for movies about 'women achievers' set in the past. A canny manager of her own image and naturally suspicious of labels, Armstrong did not always welcome the term period film director and over the course of her career at times minimised her connection to the genre. On occasion she has justified her choice to helm historically set projects via means that don't invoke a generic label, intimating, for example, that her choice has been driven by the fact that a number of good stories simply happen to be set in the past (Shirley 2011).
9 Screen Australia; the movie is also one of ten blockbuster movies produced between 2000 and 2015, by which is meant a movie with a budget of over A$50 million (Ryan and Goldsmith 2017: 9).
10 Ranked 15th by Screen Australia.
11 With the exception of a concert video Armstrong directed after *Starstruck*, called *Hard to Handle: Bob Dylan in Concert* (1986).

4

A sensual cinema: *The Last Days of Chez Nous, Unfolding Florence: The Many Lives of Florence Broadhurst, Women He's Undressed*

How might cinema engage all the human senses, in addition to those of sight and hearing? The past two decades have seen a groundswell of work by scholars such as Jennifer Barker (2009), Elena del Río (2014), Laura Marks (2002), and Vivienne Sobchack (1992; 2004) exploring film's capacity to communicate via senses of touch, tactility, taste, smell, temperature, movement, gravity, and propulsion. Recent histories of movie-going reception and exhibition have noted cinema's multisensorial aspects; examinations have canvassed mid-century technologies like smell-o-vision; multisensorial, live, event, experiential, and edible cinemas (Atkinson and Kennedy 2016; Velasco et al. 2018; Bradley 2016); and silent cinema (Gunning 2018; Gunning 2015; Burch 1990). Common to all of these is an interest in movie-going experiences exceeding the boundaries of vision and sometimes the auditorium, occasionally made available through the inclusion of interactive components such as eating, smelling, and drinking (Atkinson and Kennedy 2016: 139–40).

In the history of film theory, affective and sensorial investigations into how audiences are touched and affected by moving images in capacities that exceed narrow conceptions of the visual rose to prominence in the waning of psychoanalytic explorations of cinema. These theorists were strongly influenced by theorists of the emotions who emphasised the physical quality in emotions like fear, joy, and excitement and sometimes the leakage of these emotions into verbal language.[1] Where cinema theorists writing in the 1970s and 1980s understood cinema-going as a primarily visual experience (and secondarily aural one), from the 1990s scholars began emphasising the role of other senses to produce meaning and pleasure, often working in concert with neighbouring emotions, like fear, disgust, surprise, and delight. Though cinema's emotional and physical components had been recognised before, for example in research into melodrama, horror, and other 'body genres' (Doane 1987; Williams 2000), the post-1990s emphasis brought new methodological *gravitas* to what eventually got referred to as the 'affective turn'. As Vivian Sobchack has identified, the human body 'lives vision always in cooperation and significant exchange with other sensorial means of access to the world' (2004: 59). She writes:

> our vision is always already 'fleshed out'. Even at the movies our vision and hearing are informed and given meaning by our other modes of sensory access to the world: our capacity not only to see and to hear but also to touch, to smell, to taste, and always to proprioceptively feel our weight, dimension, gravity, and movement in the world. (2004: 60)

This chapter examines the sensorial aspects of Armstrong's movies: the colour, texture, patterning, and design elements more broadly, and sensual aspects of taste and smell, and communicates their centrality to Armstrong's filmmaking. The chapter explores Armstrong's own valuing of such elements, her prioritising of them via various production practices and choices, and the likely impact of such choices for audiences. Costuming and design form the literal subjects of two of Armstrong's biographical documentaries, which are *about* designers: *Women He's Undressed* and *Unfolding Florence*. This chapter makes use of an eclectic range of theories, including writing by Laura Marks, Rudolph Arnheim, Ben Highmore (on food), and Stella Bruzzi (on costume) in order to shed light on Armstrong's unique approach. The chapter largely focuses on Armstrong's films which best foreground these aspects,

The Last Days of Chez Nous and the two experimental documentaries, *Unfolding Florence* and *Women He's Undressed*.

Designing Armstrong

Although Armstrong is obviously known as a director, an interest in, and experience with design is threaded through her career right from the very start. As a young person, Armstrong loved literature, photography, art, and theatre; she enrolled in the four-year-long Swinburne art school course with the intention of being a production designer. In 1968 there was no dedicated NIDA (National Institute of Dramatic Art) course and Swinburne offered opportunities to study production design as part of their new film and television degree. Armstrong's first year at Swinburne was occupied with general art and design as well as photography, stop-motion animation, and costume design. Swinburne had limited money and equipment, and, from Armstrong's point of view, may have opted to delay students' access to filmmaking equipment out of financial necessity (Shirley 2011). This perhaps circuitous approach meant that she took a long time to find her pathway to film directing, but in her mind, it was time well spent (Shirley 2011).

By the time she enrolled at the national film school, Armstrong knew she wanted to be a director; but even after graduating from the school, design continued to be central. She gained experience in the art department for other directors' movies, including *The Removalists* (Tom Jeffrey 1975), and she served as art director for *The Trespassers* (John Duigan 1976) and *Promised Woman* (Tom Cowan 1975). In interviews, Armstrong tends to foreground the centrality of pre-production processes of set and costume over other processes such as scriptwriting. These are often the first aspects of a film that she will talk about, suggesting she is at ease expressing opinions about these aspects and regards them as key to the filmmaking process. Brainstorming about design seems to provide an imaginative way for her into a project and is how she first begins envisioning what a project will be like.

Debi Enker's description of the process through which Armstrong became attached to *Mrs. Soffel* is illustrative of Armstrong's method in this regard (1985). Design is the first production element mentioned in the article. According to Enker:

> Armstrong explains: 'Our major concept was to make it look like a black and white film. For me, the strongest image was blood on the snow. There was really to be no colour in the overall design until the blood red on the snow. I didn't want it to be a romantic sort of past, because it wasn't a romantic time at all.' (Enker 1985: 28)

Interest in film's expressive potential beyond its technological capacities as a recording instrument has philosophical antecedents stretching back to the first third of the twentieth century, to theories of Eisenstein, the Russian formalists, and others. Writing in the 1930s, Rudolph Arnheim elaborated film's aesthetic potency to offer something important and unique, midway between human perception and technologically precise recording. A strong advocate for silent film, Arnheim disliked the realism which he believed sound added; he felt the addition of sound brought the mechanical copy closer to a mere reproduction of reality (Elsaesser and Hagener 2010: 22). In contrast, silent film could achieve an artistic effect and productively '*take liberties* with space and time' (Arnheim 1957: 24; emphasis added), which Arnheim valued. He wrote: 'People who contemptuously refer to the camera as an automatic recording machine must be made to realize that even in the simplest photographic reproduction of a perfectly simple object, a *feeling for its nature* is required which is quite beyond any mechanical operation' (1957: 11; emphasis added).

Armstrong's approach to set design in *Mrs. Soffel* expressed in the interview with Enker, described above, evidences the 'taking liberty' mentioned by Arnheim; her identification of the significance of the red colour indicates her grasp or 'feeling' for the 'nature' of the blood in the climactic ending scene; in other words the relevance of the blood and its ability (through the focus on colour) to convey the trauma, defeat, and death that ensues at the climax of *Mrs. Soffel* (to which the discussion with Enker refers). In this moment of planning described by Enker, Armstrong reveals her understanding that identifying the core elements of the scene and designing in such a way to bring focus to them, was key. As Arnheim might say, Armstrong's task, like that of cinema, was not to reproduce its subject with mechanical accuracy but rather 'in the higher, aesthetic sense of the term – render its essentials faithfully' (Arnheim 1957: 162).

Arnheim's language may strike some as romantic or essentialist. Yet at the heart of his conjecture is an idea of great resonance for Armstrong's work, which concerns cinema's capacity to communicate the core of a given situation, object, or character, through essentially non-verbal means – through sight and sound and other means outlined in this chapter's introduction. Arnheim's belief that film can highlight and consequently draw our attention to those 'qualities of things that we would miss in a mechanical recording' (Thomson-Jones 2008: 10) would seem to have been written with Armstrong's production processes in mind.

It is enlightening to explore Armstrong's account of pre-production undertaken for *The Last Days of Chez Nous* in light of Arnheim's ideas. In her description of the pre-production process, Armstrong tells how two television monitors were put in proximity to each other in order to test what Lisa Harrow (who was auditioning for the role of Beth) and Kerry Fox (who was testing for Vicki) would look like together; Armstrong thought to set up the monitors because Harrow and Fox were unable to test together at the same time and Armstrong needed to assess whether they could plausibly pass as sisters. Janet Patterson was asked to ameliorate the semblance of sisterliness, and she advised colouring the women's hair the identical shade of red (Shirley 2011).

Like Armstrong's description of designing for *Mrs. Soffel*, this anecdote about *Last Days* may at first glance appear largely of practical significance: the nuts and bolts solving of a minor pre-production logistical problem. My conviction is that scrutinising such moments can shed light on Armstrong's working methods and indicate the level of detail at which Armstrong and her team are accustomed to working, and moreover what matters for Armstrong and what she aims to achieve. In addition to serving as a practical solution, the co-situating of the monitors gives a sense of the angle from which thorny problems are addressed and the centrality of non-verbal sensual matters to Armstrong's considerations.

In this story, hair colour is *not* irrelevant. Attention to this issue results in the impression of physical resemblance; the impression of physical resemblance produces character plausibility; character plausibility may foster affective responses, which may themselves lead to filmmaking success. Success in this case requires a working process and method to establish the relation between characters, a perception of their essential nature, and ability to communicate this via small but precise and sensual details.

One of the challenges for film practitioners who emphasise such sensorial aspects, as Armstrong does, are the physical limitations of the film medium itself; the majority of cinema going has not historically involved literal touching or taste or indeed much physical movement. A good deal of work on the sensorial has attended to cinema's ability to communicate the impression of the sensorial and/or the ways in which images and sounds – the bread and butter of cinematic communication – may affect the spectator in embodied or physical ways.

Film theorists have attempted to delineate new perceptual approaches that may produce such responses. In Laura Marks's term, the haptic is an extended sense of visuality that emphasises film's ability to engage other senses – in her formulation, this is typically the sense of touch. The haptic is the 'combination of tactile, kinaesthetic, and proprioceptive functions, the way we experience touch both on the surface of and inside our bodies' (2002: 2). Haptic perception differs from optical perception, in that there is no 'object' of the haptic look; rather there are 'dynamic subjectivities' between the image and viewer (2002: 3). Haptic perception is embodied and multisensorial; while optical viewing affects only the audience member's eye, haptic perception affects the sense of touch: 'it enables an embodied perception: the viewer responding to the video as to another body, and to the screen as another skin' (2002: 4).

Overall, my impression is that Marks's clarifications shed light on the haptic as a perceptual practice rather than spelling out in literal terms a haptic cinematographic approach or what, for example, a haptic referent should look like. She writes 'haptic looking tends to rest on the surface of its object rather than to plunge into depth, not to distinguish form so much as to discern texture' (2002: 8) and cautions that '[a]ny out-of-focus or low-resolution image is not necessarily haptic' (2002: 8–9). Jennifer Barker shares with Marks a conviction that thinking about cinema requires a paradigm shift to show how 'touch is a "style of being" shared by both film and viewer'; like Marks, her aim is to open 'the possibility of cinema as an *intimate* experience and of our relationship with cinema as a close connection, rather than as a distant experience of observation, which the notion of cinema as a purely visual medium presumes' (2; emphasis, Barker's).

Barker's and Marks's comments are thought-provoking, but abstract. Their relation to visual materials is suggested rather than proscribed, leaving their potential for application open-ended. They indicate forms of audience engagement that films may elicit, including those of Armstrong. In what follows, I will explore Armstrong's movies through these frameworks in an attempt to identify concrete moments where such ideas apply.

The Last Days of Chez Nous (1992)

From a script by Australian author Helen Garner, *The Last Days of Chez Nous* is a contemporary-set realist drama about potentially large and affecting events, including the breakdown of a marriage and consequential dissolution of a household, a changing and possibly cooling relationship between sisters, and a reconciliation between parent and adult child. At the centre of most of these developments is middle-aged, middle-class writer Beth. Beth (Lisa Harrow) is the central organiser and caregiver in a household full of free spirits; these comprise her daughter Annie (Miranda Otto), her younger and more impulsive sister Vicki (Kerry Fox), her French husband JP (played by Bruno Ganz), and a boarder, Tim (Kiri Paramore). Beth aims for the neat and tidy and is thus totally unprepared when she returns from a road trip and finds her husband and sister have fallen in love. Although the breakdown of the marital relationship between Beth and JP has been identified as central to the film (Buckmaster 2015), the film goes to great lengths not to point fingers or apportion blame. In my mind, the movie is also very much interested in Beth's experience – what happens when the lid blows off and control is lost.

The films opens with Vicki slouching back into town after an unsuccessful love affair overseas. Vicki's red suitcase is the first sign of her that audiences see, as it enters the frame of a knee-level shot and the camera (helmed by Geoffrey Simpson) moves to track the suitcase as Vicki drags it behind her down the street. Vicki's face remains unseen as she pushes her way through the front gate of the row house and continues to walk away from the camera. She calls out but no one answers, suggesting perhaps she is either early or late or her arrival is not anticipated. Still not showing her face, the camera wanders inside the home up to a dark wooden table on which a home-made cake with the words 'welcome home' clarify the state of affairs. Vicki knifes unceremoniously into the cake, carving out a generous portion and proceeding to stuff it into her mouth. This is the first glance audiences have of Vicki's face as she walks idly around the kitchen, glances at its walls and in particular, at a pin-up board. She plucks a photo of a handsome young man from off of the board and rips it to shreds, walks up the narrow set of steps, and retches.

From this opening scene, several things become clear. From the cake on the table, it is clear that Vicki's arrival is indeed anticipated and desired, but perhaps a bit mistimed. The pin-up board indicates traces of middle-class lives well lived: there are photos of people with smiling faces, tourist maps and other holiday mementos, what appears to be a copied-out recipe, and a newspaper cutting announcing a writing prize awarded to someone named 'Elizabeth' (clearly the 'Beth' at the centre of the story). From Vicki we gain a sense that she is familiar with the home and somewhat curious about its contents, mildly irritated (evident in her ripping up of the photo), and physically unwell. The hurried, grabbing of the cake and minor retching when ascending the stairs, the slow steps and exhaustion all combine to convey a sense of someone who is ruled by her body at this point in time, immune to politer rules of society, and/or sufficiently familiar with the home inhabitants not to wait for them before carving into the cake. When Vicki finds a double bed upstairs, she lies down, relieved, but almost immediately, jumps up, runs off-screen to a bathroom, and vomits.

Shortly after this scene, the family – Beth, JP, and Beth's daughter, Annie – return home. JP prepares dinner and basic qualities of the household are quickly established: it is progressive (with JP taking charge of domestic matters, such as cooking), values humour and play (Beth, Vicki, and the nearly grown Annie play with children's toys while seated on the floor; JP and Annie play a hat-throwing game; the prospective boarder, Tim, is directly asked whether he has a sense of humour), and subscribes largely to middle-class aspirationalism (Beth, Vicki, and Annie all delight in making fun of working-class 'sheilas' when they mimic the 'rough' accents of their pretend alter egos, Cheryl, Chantelle, and Tiffany Butterworth). Tension between the characters is also introduced: JP criticises Beth's need for order, turns away from her in bed, and scorns the game about the Butterworths.

The family journeys to Vicki and Beth's parents' house for dinner. There are striking contrasts between the woman-dominated home Beth heads and the patriarchally ruled home of the parents; in an argument with Beth and Vicki's mother, JP advocates that mealtimes ought to be communal and bemoans the Australian practice of buffet eating. A momentary realignment of the divisions occurs around dessert, when all the women join to decry Beth's father's (Bill Hunter) pouring of cream on his raspberries (for what audiences understand to be health reasons), and JP leaps to the father's defence.

While all films engage senses of sight and sound, *The Last Days of Chez Nous* is unique in its communication of meaning through aspects that call on all five human senses. Via heightened attention to elements of colour, texture, patterning, and design (especially the design of the house), *Last Days* engages senses of sight and touch. Hearing is engaged in interesting and innovative ways, both through extra-diegetic sound in the original and subtly modulated jazz soundtrack and via on-screen musical themes. Most uniquely, *Last Days* activates senses of smell and taste in multiple scenes involving food, cooking, eating, and in the varied and complex assigning of meaning to food. All these sensory elements join to communicate character attributes, story themes, and other narrative information.

Armstrong establishes complex family dynamics rapidly and effectively largely through the framing or scripting around a range of seemingly unimportant objects, like cake or cream (mentioned above). *Last Days* communicates that the small and sensual details form the matter of relationships and are the instrument through which they are measured. Raffaele Caputo has stated that 'another defining element of the relationships is the concentration on little details and objects as indicators of what is going on emotionally' (1992: 8). The clear purpose of such objects is to express immediately and without words entrenched family dynamics about love, protection, care, control, and the valuing of hospitality. A major question posed by the film at this early point, is whether and how characters can change when caught within familial networks that are simultaneously supportive and constricting.

In an attempt to provide an answer to this question, Beth invites her father to take a journey with her into the outback. A thirty-minute-long sequence in the middle of the film establishes the progression of the two different narrative strands: Beth on the road with her curmudgeonly father, and Vicki at home with JP, Annie, and Tim. At the outset, things don't go very well between Beth and her father. The latter character is scripted and performed as critical, miserly, stubborn, ungenerous, incapable of expressing emotions, and inflexible. This is indicated by countless scenes and comments, such as his decision to keep his watch set on Eastern standard time; his bringing of his own water from home; his insisting that he and Beth eat the entire bag of oranges as they approach the state border (rather than having to 'wastefully' surrender them to quarantine authorities). His crippling critical tendencies are in view when he admonishes his daughter for petty things like not knowing how to put on the handbrake and for eating too much. He says, 'It's a wonder you don't get fat, the amount you eat between meals.'

Painful scenes between Beth and her father contrast sharply with scenes back at Beth's house, where spontaneous play is supported and which appears conducive to the expression of emotion and empathy. Conversations demonstrate Vicki's growing understanding of JP's feelings as a non-English-speaking migrant living in a foreign country, and his realisation that she has had an abortion. In a memorable scene, JP wears a sieve for a makeshift hat and joins Vicki to frolic around the house. Scenes such as this are a joyous relief from the tension between Beth and JP and between Beth and her father.

As the film cuts between these two developing threads, Vicki's and Beth's respective lives remain un-intertwined; the cross-cutting largely accommodates longish, discrete sequences of events. In one exceptional moment, editing brings the two sisters' story worlds together with that of their father. The camera shows Beth sitting up in the hotel bed, writing in her diary. On the television soundtrack, we hear a man's voice, saying 'push'. The escalating screams of a woman's voice are heard, and a point of view shot from Beth's perspective shows the blurry head of a baby, on the television, being born. There is a reverse shot of Lisa Harrow's face, taking in the TV programme. The next shot returns to the television, only this time pans away from it across the living room where Vicki is watching the television, sobbing and rocking gently back and forth. The sequence includes Bill Hunter in the hotel room next to Beth's, who raises his gaze from a newspaper to see the same TV movie on his hotel television; he rises and turns the channel to a game of cricket. Vicki's pain recalling her recent abortion contrasts with a final shot of Beth's contented face, for whom the achievement of producing children is – in marked contrast – obviously a happy memory.

Where previously the film had drawn a picture of extreme closeness between Vicki and Beth, this triply connected sequence indicates what is in fact the fracturing of their relationship; with this sequence, Armstrong communicates their different existential positions with respect to weighty matters of birth and parenthood. Felicity Collins has interpreted the father's reaction as a patriarchal censoring (1999: 60); additionally, it importantly functions to distinguish the two sisters, and to mark the pivotal moment after which everything changes.

In the house as Vicki continues to cry, JP appears with a bowl of soup; the two kiss and their romantic relationship begins. On the highway, a tentative peace between Beth and her father arrives when they share a bowl of ice cream at a roadside café. The remaining screen time is spent working out the emotional and practical logistics of Beth and JP's separation. JP and Vicki move into a barren-looking, bare-walled, inauspicious-appearing apartment. While the futures for all three remain unclear at the end, the movie concludes with a focus on Beth. Seated on the steps at the front of her home, she sees something in the distance that catches her eye. A smile creeps across her face, she rises and strides forth briskly from the house. The fast-paced, upbeat 'Donna Lee' by Charlie Parker (performed by the Groovematics) is heard on the soundtrack. With this song, the movie conveys optimism about Beth's future.

To return to Arnheim, he understood that in real life, people marshal different forms of attention depending on their individual circumstances. He believed that people see

> only so much of the objects surrounding [them] as necessary for [their] purpose. If a man is standing at the counter of a haberdasher's shop, the salesman will presumably pay less attention to the customer's facial expression than to the kind of tie he is wearing (so as to

guess his taste) … But when the same man enters his office his secretary will doubtless pay less attention to his tie than to his facial expression (so as to know what sort of temper he is in). (Arnheim 1957: 42)

While Arnheim draws his examples from the world of commerce (and not the home or hotel room, as Armstrong does), the triple point of view scene just described similarly indicates the different meaning people may ascribe to the same object or event. For Beth, the birth movie is experienced as poignant and joyous; for Beth's father, uninteresting; and for Vicki, the movie brings pain. What Armstrong accomplishes with the triple telling, Arnheim might say, is guiding the spectator's attention via framing or other formal choice (42); when the attention is guided, 'things that previously remained unnoticed are the more striking because the object itself as a whole appears strange and unusual. The spectator is thus brought to see something familiar as something new. At this moment he becomes capable of true observation' (44).

With Armstrong's direction, scenes and events such as Beth's father's bringing his own water on the trip, the joyless and hurried eating of oranges, and the triply connected sequence centred around the television movie about birth, bring new insight to audiences about familiar relationship aspects.

Sound and taste

In *Last Days*, sound functions as a bridge between isolated individuals and is the metric through which relationships may be measured. Changing as moods alter and circumstances progress, the non-diegetic jazz-inflected soundtrack is a subtle but insistent backdrop through much of the movie. On occasion it is punctuated by tonally contrasting music, such as baroque-inflected harpsichord music (audible at the end of the dinner at Beth's parents' home and when Beth learns of JP and Vicki's affair), and like 'The Loved One' performed by the Australian band The Loved Ones (heard when Annie and Vicki play in the house, after Beth leaves). Music is a medium for non-verbal expression, as in the use of harmonica when Beth and her father are on their road trip, and via the short burst of fast-paced, major-key, harpsichord music heard when Annie and Tim are at the beginning of their relationship, and ride together on a bicycle.

Music plays a significant role indicating Beth's moods in particular. Right after JP tells Beth of his feelings for Vicki, she begins destroying the family bathroom; accompanying these actions is a dramatic-sounding, emphatic, somewhat slow-paced, minor-key piece of harpsichord music (as mentioned above). The piece resembles the major-key music heard only a few minutes earlier in the film, when Annie and Tim ride off on the bicycle, because both make use of the same instruments; but heard here in a minor key, the music and accompanying effects could not be more different.

Thematically, melophilia is an indication of a character's likeability and possibly sensual capacity. Music is important to JP, who keeps what Vicki calls his 'daggy French music' hidden; Vicki's acknowledging the importance of this signals an advance in their relationship. The actual production (or playing) of music is important to several characters, including Beth's daughter Annie and the boarder Tim, who spend hours companionably practising the same piece at the piano. Their relationship is tracked via the progress Annie makes with a ragtime tune they play with increasing proficiency. Tim is identified as a jazz fan; his knowledge and enthusiasm about the early American performer Jelly Roll Morton indicates that he is quite quirky and likeable.

In addition to qualities of the aural, another important means of communication in Last Days is food. Food both serves to metaphorically unite characters and shed light on their differences, in ways that sometimes appear gendered and often culturally specific. Vicki's swift, gluttonous gorging on a giant slice of cake early in the movie indicates both her unthinking selfishness and her lack of inhibition at home in her sister's house, an approach that is also taken by Beth when she cuts into the special French cheese JP has been saving.

These paired consumption events (of the cake and the cheese) bring to light shared traits between the two women. As for the men: JP's attachment to and defending of the cheese indicates the value he places on the sensual experience of consuming it, his connection through the food to his country of birth, and his position as an outsider within the Australian family who doesn't understand its importance to him. JP's strong emotions about this object contrast sharply with the attitude of Beth's Anglo-Australian father's, whose preference is for a sterile packet of chips.

On the road trip, the oranges which Beth and her father obligatorily consume before passing through the quarantine checkpoint on their driving trip clearly express the veneer of duty and suffering in their relationship that is wholly absent from the developing relationship between JP and Vicki, who (in contrast) prepare a beautiful tray of green and purple grapes, apples, and bananas just prior to dancing together. While JP refuses to accept Beth's extension of an invitation to dinner, he expresses his feelings for Vicki by bringing her soup, and they share their first kiss over this bowl of broth. Although Beth's father criticises Beth for stuffing food into her mouth in frustration and for eating between meals, what reconciliation they are able to achieve is through their sharing of ice cream, when he offers to help her eat a second scoop she has been given in the roadside café (but has not asked for). When the waitress brings two scoops to the table, Beth protests, 'I only wanted one.' The waitress answers, 'Well, I thought it looked a bit lonely', anthropomorphising the dessert and positioning it as both a conduit for human emotions and a revised relationship between Beth and her father.

Beth and her father are in dark shadow in this scene, shown in a two-shot, with the bright glare of the outback behind them. There is a pause, the waitress leaves. 'Hey', says the father, 'I'll give you a hand.' An overhead shot captures the two scoops in the bright silver dish, arranged with two pink and brown wafer cookies; beneath the dish is a cheery red and white checked tablecloth.

The shot is unusual on account of the camera positioning (which is quite close), its wordlessness, and the slow and deliberate division of the two scoops, by the father's spoon, before he digs in to one of the scoops to take a bite. For audiences, it communicates a break in the arguments and communicates, as Arnheim would say, the familiar as new.

In the above-cited examples, the meaning given to food, and how it is consumed, is diverse and complex. Many of the examples clearly emphasise the significance of the sensual: the eating and enjoyment of a diversity of foods that are rich in colour, smell, texture, savouriness, and cultural value. At the same time, perhaps more subtly, the film also forwards an idea that access to the sensual in such moments is fleeting, unable to be guaranteed, frequently repressed (like emotions), and thus important not to take for granted. The family's concerted efforts to deny Beth's father a dollop of cream for his raspberries (in the interests of 'protecting his health') is a prime example of such censoring, to which, we might assume, the father's irascibility is a response.

In 'Bitter after Taste: Affect, Food, and Social Aesthetics', Ben Highmore promotes a scholarly approach to social relations that would attend to the 'sticky entanglements of substances and feelings, of matter and affect [that] are central to our contact with the world' (2010: 119). Social aesthetics is the term he coins to represent the cross-modal and synesthetic investigations into sensate perception, which include experiences of bodies and senses. Highmore is especially interested in what role food may play in mitigating culture clashes between different races and social groups. Where a superficial investigation may see food reproducing old rivalries, Highmore appreciates the 'complexity of these intermingling registers' and their ability to 'guard against predictable effects and affects' (135). He acknowledges the centrality of taste to social struggles and declares it to be both 'an orchestration of the sensible, a way of ordering and demeaning, of giving value and taking it away' and 'the very basis of culture . . . From one angle at least, social struggle is struggle through, in, and about taste' (126).

I have spent some time on these aspects because, in my mind, *Last Days*'s central positioning of food and eating stands as an exception to the rest of Armstrong's work, where eating is a drudgery and preparing food a burden that women almost exclusively shoulder. Scenes throughout *The Story of Kerry, Josie and Diana* (discussed in the next chapter) indicate that providing food is what women are obliged to do for various (often male) family members. In *High Tide* (also discussed in the next chapter), Lilli receives a pair of dressed chickens as a raffle prize but is flummoxed by what to do with them and gives them away. In the dining scenes set in the prison in *Mrs. Soffel* and amongst the well-to-do in *My Brilliant Career*, eating is associated with social conformity and emotional restriction; scenes of Kate Soffel and Sybylla Melvyn seated at a table are formal and pleasureless. As discussed here, *Last Days* understands both the historical association of food preparation with women's labour and food consumption with bodily surveillance. But in addition, it recognises positive connections between food, love, and culture and its powerful potential as source of sensual solace.

House as character

The production component that has received the most attention in *Last Days*, in interview materials and critical appraisals, is the set design. Sometimes referred to as production design, art direction, or film architecture, set design has received scholarly consideration through auteur-oriented and historical *mise-en-scène* analyses. Set design has often been conceived as support to the overarching narrative of a film, with the paradoxical result that the success of a design may be evaluated according to its invisibility and capacity to go unnoticed. Some scholars have claimed that set design is one of the more underexamined industrial components of film production (Bergfelder et al. 2007: 13. See also Affron and Affron 1995). Like other industrial components, set design may be judged according to internal industrial metrics, such as a designer's capacity to deliver on time and within budget.

Sets obviously comprise physical components including architecture, whose brief is delivering humans through space. In the case of film, the architecture is obviously not experienced in an embodied way but remains at the level of the visual. Theorists such as Charles Tashiro, Peter Wollen, and Giuliana Bruno have speculated about the extent to which a film set can deliver an architecture-like experience and, through this, the impression of embodiment and kinetic movement through space. All this is achieved via the interaction of camera within the fabricated space of a film set, sometimes in excess or in lieu of what is directly expressed in a narrative (Tashiro 1998).

At their most basic, sets produce the historical, geographical, and social 'look' of a given story, the unspoken sociocultural context which conveys characters' social class, familial status, and emotional outlook as well as a host of other details. Sets convey what Bourdieu termed the *habitus* of a character (or characters): the physical embodiment of sociocultural capital that presents as 'taste' (Bourdieu 1977).

In is difficult to overemphasise the importance of the house in *Last Days*, where almost the entirety of the movie's events take place. In Graham Shirley's words, the house was a *character*, indicating his understanding of the house's value in the overall world of the story (2011). Critics praised the film for its attention to geographic detail. Luke Buckmaster noted the movie's ability to 'follow its characters with close geographical and emotional proximity' (Buckmaster 2015).

Last Days takes place in a tiny, cramped, Sydney terrace house; interview comments indicate Armstrong's understanding of the challenges she faced to make it visually interesting and a space her crew could work in. She describes the process by which Peter Lawless (the location finder) found the house, cinematographer Geoffrey Simpson viewed it, and designer Janet Patterson devised colour schemes for it. According to Armstrong, Patterson proposed to paint the walls dark grey to offset the 'jewel' colours of the respective female leads' blue eyes, auburn hair, and pale skin. The result was a warm, inviting, beautiful, richly patterned, and textured space (Shirley 2011).

Beth's home (the 'chez nous' of the movie's title) flouts what Marks has termed a 'maximization of the visible' (2002: 91); it exudes colour, light, pattern, and texture, all of which become evident within the film's first two minutes, and which contrast vividly with Beth's parents' home (with its antiseptic white walls and orderly and sparse decorations) and with the sterile-appearing apartment where JP and Vicki move at the film's end. In Felicity Collins's words, 'Armstrong's attentive *mise-en-scène* relishes small intimacies realised visually and performatively through objects and movements, faces and actions, rather than explanatory dialogue and narrative logic' (1999: 58).

In the streetscape leading up to Beth's home in the film's opening moments, audiences note the tactile patterns on back-alley fences and crumbling bricks that lead up to the terrace house, the faded striped outdoor drop-down shades, and the Italianate red, blue, and white floor tiles around the entrance. Once inside, they see a house crammed with furniture, ornaments, books, patterned rugs, toys, and all manner of friendly clutter. When Vicki makes her way upstairs, her face is shrouded in darkness as she enters the first upstairs room. Stepping forward, light enters the scene, her face brightens, and she smiles. The camera pulls back as she continues to walk towards it; as she spins on her heel and exits the room, the camera continues to track back, revealing an intriguing space full of glass mobiles and ornaments hanging from the ceiling, patterned bags hanging off the back of a door, an Alexander Calder-inspired black silhouette affixed to a wall, a wooden dresser supporting assorted jewellery, ceramic ornaments, and candles, and a wooden fireplace with another pin-up board. Like the rest of the house, the room is inviting and warm. There is an invitation to touch the ornaments inside.

Marks's description of haptic perception reveals detachment from abstract navigational methods with which optical vision tends to be associated: 'touching, not mastering' is the quality that is required when bodies attempt to move through 'close-range spaces', like snow or sand (2002: xii). These are the types of spaces that Vicki first encounters when she, pregnant and unwell and dragging her heavy suitcase, returns home and enters the house; she appears bewildered, necessitating a navigation that is both particular and requires updating with every step she takes.

Though audiences first encounter these tactile qualities through Vicki's point of view and not Beth's, it is worth remembering that the house is an extension of Beth's personality: she has created it. The film thus complicates and resists reifying the varying personalities within what could appear to be a rigidly defined love triangle via their imbricated and overlapping relation to the shared space.

Over the course of *Last Days*, the house is the constant which all three main characters ironically end up leaving. Vicki moves to an antiseptic-looking apartment in a relationship with JP (which, he suggests, may not last long). Beth strides forth from the family home on to the street, and perhaps in the direction of a spire she has expressed curiosity about earlier in the story. The sisterly relationship has suffered a huge blow, and it is not at all clear that that will be repaired. *Last Days* is a forensic examination of the dynamics of change in human relationships and how domestic minutiae – food, music, clutter, and further house elements – form the vocabulary to express this. *Last Days* is finally a story 'about' many characters and different relationships; its most important accomplishment may be its training of the audience to see the familiar as new and thus to become capable of true observation.

Unfolding Florence: The Many Lives of Florence Broadhurst (2006)

Unfolding Florence is the first of Armstrong's pair of experimental biographical documentaries and is about Australian designer Florence Broadhurst, an original and 'Aussie doyenne' whose innovative ideas for interior design have spread around the globe (Green 2007: 74). The documentary tells the story of

Broadhurst's life in a roughly chronological manner by means of an actor's voice, interview testimony, archival imagery, and animation. The story begins with the information that in 1977 Florence Broadhurst was violently bludgeoned to death at the age of seventy-eight, and that this murder was never solved. From here the story goes back in time and narrates from the beginning the story of Florence's life. We hear that she grew up in a small town in rural Queensland, moved to Asia and joined the world of society, dance, and drama, returned to Australia, where she rose to prominence as a wallpaper designer and became a leading figure in Sydney's high society. The film does not conceal Florence's tendency to fabricate, and references are made to her pretending to be British, and from a wealthy grazier's family (neither of which are true) – in other words the 'many lives' of the movie's title.

As the first of what would be two experimental biographical documentaries by Armstrong, *Unfolding* makes a radical departure from Armstrong's prior realist documentaries, motivated in part by finances and in part by the practical exigencies of the subject matter, that is by the fact that Broadhurst was no longer living and Armstrong possessed no live footage of her to work with. The film was thus governed by different constraints than Armstrong's prior work in documentary and new possibilities opened up (Edwards 2006: 40).

In the main, footage in the film comes from four separate sources and production processes: interview footage, silhouette-styled cut-out animated footage, archival imagery, and dramatised sequences. The range of selected interviewees includes friends and relatives (such as June Gollan and Florence's niece Phyllis Nicholson), people from the arts communities (including screen designer Kate Dagher), and graziers. Nearly all of the interviews take place in interior spaces, with the interviewees largely positioned against flat backdrops; the background designs appear coordinated with the respective clothing of the interviewees, so that colours align or complement each other. Gollan, for example, wears a pale green top and is seated against a pale brown-green chair; Dagher wears a black top and sits in front of a green floral print; Nicholson is dressed in pale mauve against a largely pink background. The result is a highly stylised, colour-choreographed *mise-en-scène* comprising a flattened out depth of field and a highlighting of patterns, colours, and shapes. This emphasis is consistent with other sets thus far discussed in this chapter, in the flattening of the image, the limiting of depth of field, and the drawing attention to pattern, texture, colour, and shape. The effect is a heightened awareness of the relationship between figure and ground, with the majority of sequences creating the impression of a compressed visual field.

The film's animations, which form the second most common source of footage, also display this visual compression or flattening. The animations – formed from a mounted digital still camera and moved around bits of paper, shot frame by frame (Avenell 2006: 71) – are hand-drawn and comprise a playful array of cut-out figures, animals, objects, arrows, angels, cows, bags of money, dates, and other objects which float or jiggle against flat-appearing, largely still backgrounds, comprised of old postcards, photographs, or film stills. In many cases, the animated figures appear to 'dance' across the backgrounds and bring an impression of liveliness and movement. Both figures and backgrounds are hand-coloured, conveying an overall impression of flatness, rather than depth, like a magnet affixed to a fridge door.[2]

William Moritz has examined the career trajectory of German artist and animator Lotte Reiniger (2012) and tracked her rise in the German entertainment industry just prior to World War Two, from aspiring actress to creator of animated silhouette shorts, to creator of feature films. Reiniger's success as an animator was based in large part on her cutting dexterity: the silhouette figures needed to be individually cut out, and Reiniger initially began to do this by cutting out silhouette portraits of stars while waiting as an actress between scenes (13).

Obviously in the digital moment, the need for such a manual process has attenuated. But there are strong visual parallels between the folk-art inspired silhouettes seen in Reiniger's work and Armstrong's, suggesting an echoing and revival of a technique bearing traces of feminist labour and form in the folk-art tradition.³

Women He's Undressed (2015)

Women He's Undressed is Armstrong's second formally experimental biographical documentary about one of the great costume designers of the classical Hollywood period. Orry-Kelly had a celebrated career and created costumes for well-known classics like *The Maltese Falcon* and *Casablanca* and for stars such as Natalie Wood, Ava Gardner, and Bette Davis; he was an openly gay Australian man and a three-time Oscar winner for *An American in Paris*, *Les Girls*, and *Some Like it Hot*. Most significantly, the movie claims he was the friend, room-mate, part-time partner in tie-making, and lover of Archie Leach/Cary Grant. Like *Unfolding Florence*, much of *Women* makes use of experimental techniques: live actors playing Orry-Kelly and deceased Hollywood movie stars; non-realist stage sets; and repurposed movie technologies, such as rear projection, that draw attention to the constructedness of the *mise-en-scène*. Like other movies discussed in this chapter, *Women He's Undressed* makes vibrant use of tactility and visual texture.

With the story of Orry-Kelly's relationship with Cary Grant, *Women* is positioned as a film with a message to tell. At the script level, the film fronts a pro-truth approach, beginning with the quote from American singer/actress Fanny Brice that opens the movie: 'Let the world know who you are, because sooner or later, if you are posing, you will forget the pose. Then where will you be?' The words of Orry-Kelly (voiced by actor Darren Gilshenan, who plays Kelly in the experimental reconstructed sequences in the film) echo this at the movie's end. When asked what he wants at his funeral, Orry-Kelly answers 'The truth . . . just the truth.' *Women* is constructed as an investigation into the *truth* about Orry-Kelly's personal life, and much is made of Kelly's courage not succumbing to heteronormative expectations of the day. The movie aims to bring to light the contributions of this forgotten Australian artist as well as the unstated rules governing professional behaviour in the classical Hollywood period, where certain forms of relationships were not tolerated. A shot early on shows the sweeping light of a lighthouse, forwarding the idea that the film will be revelatory. Orry-Kelly is celebrated for being open about his life, and for his honesty in being, as Gilshenan puts it, 'never too good at masking what I think or who I am for that matter'. Orry voices these words in the first introductory four minutes of the film while seated in a rowboat (mentioned in this book's introduction), in an effort to imagine what Cary Grant would have said about him.

While the movie sees itself as the voice of truth, it is also a concerted and sustained celebration of artifice and the performativity of especially clothing to create new identities. Many of the movie interviewees attest to this. Marc Eliot for example says about Kelly, 'If you look the part, you can become the part.' Costume designer Ann Roth uses similar ideas to describe what costume designers can achieve: 'Keep looking in the mirror . . . and suddenly another *being* is there. It sounds like magic . . . but it isn't, it's real . . . you can do it with a shoulder pad . . . or a beer belly. Something that removes the actor from himself.' Kelly's own professional accomplishments, audiences hear, created precisely such performative, sartorial transformations, as for example with Natalie Wood, who played the role of a stripper in *Gypsy* (1962); according to *Women*, due to the clothing Kelly designed, Wood conveyed the impression of an eroticism that was dominating and forceful, in spite of Wood's own small stature (Wood was actually only 5 foot 2 inches tall). For the black-and-white film *Jezebel* (1938), Kelly's design for the scandalous 'red' dress Bette Davis wore in the film was similarly so affecting, it fully conveyed the impression of red in spite of the fact that the film was shot in black and white (Leonard Maltin, quoted in *Women He's Undressed*).

In addition to detailing these qualities in Kelly's own creative output, the film demonstrates a commitment to artifice in its own style. As said, much of the film makes use of experimental technique; the impression of texture is created through the incorporation of clips from movies that Kelly worked on and from the integration of new, highly stylised footage.

For example, within the first two minutes of the film, the camera tracks the slowly, rhythmically flowing rose- and salmon-coloured dresses of eight women who appear to act as pall-bearers on a grassy hilltop. A shot from above reveals the actor who plays Orry-Kelly, lying – not in a coffin – but in a red rowboat. The colours of the women's dresses are echoed in the colours of the red electrician's tape that is across the actor's mouth, and in Kelly's pink carnation that is in his buttonhole. Still walking in dreamy slow motion, the women exit the frame and the opening credits begin to appear. Shortly after this opening, there is a scene of a young Orry-Kelly positioned in a rowboat against a free-standing wall panel with a sheet patterned with the ocean draped over it. The camera draws back to reveal the panel is positioned on a theatre stage, on the back wall of which moving images of the ocean are projected. The set-up marks the artifice of the image and, as before, overloads the *mise-en-scène* with tactility and texture. Later in the movie, film clips focus on women Kelly dressed (Bette Davis; Natalie Wood; Marilyn Monroe; Angela Lansbury) in various sumptuous, dazzling, improbable costumes. The clips draw attention to the texture and material of fabric (furs, sequins), its movement (the shimmering of a gown), and often the movement of an actor through space (Bette Davis's drop to the bottom of a frame).

Bill Nichols (2017) has described the differences between the image/sound relationship in expository documentary and the relationship in narrative feature films. Where narrative fiction tends to present coherence of space and uses editing to convey this, documentary is not beholden to such rules and will tend to organise imagery around a centring commentary or voice-over. The result is an opportunity for documentary imagery to come 'loose' from the world of the anchoring story, to be fanciful, imaginative, and – in the case of this movie – textural. While Gilshenan narrates, a diversity of images combine to show Kelly in various theatrical settings or rowing outdoors on a body of water. Drawings and sketches by Kelly are included, along with archival images that correspond to Kelly's experiences (such as an ocean liner departing; street and club images from New York in the 1920s). Movie stills and clips from films he contributed to are also incorporated.

Film production culture in the Fordist period of classical Hollywood during which Orry-Kelly worked was typified by a hierarchical and inflexible approach to labour through which industry workers tended to be contracted to one of the major studios and a hierarchy of prestige and payment separated 'above the line' roles of screenwriter, producer, director, and actors from 'below the line' roles (pretty much everybody else). Film studies histories have historically tended to focus on above-the-line roles and overlooked many others, though through renewed interest in the contributions of women, there is some evidence this focus is shifting.

Women is fully aware of this hierarchy, celebrates the labour that has previously gone unseen, in both scripting (the story that it chooses to focus on) and in the texture of the images that accompany that story. There is a tongue-in-cheek questioning of the value placed on those above-the-line roles to the neglect of others. Thus Kelly's opening words referring to himself as a 'hem-stitcher' ironise and draw attention to the tendency to relegate the frequently feminised roles of design to the bottom, below those of director and producer. In bringing attention to the tactility of Orry-Kelly's own contributions, *Women* elevates the once debased specialty of costume design. Audiences are alerted to the labour, knowledge, and expertise he brought to the role to create what at times was meant to be an invisible product.

Taking a scholarly step back from the film, it is apparent in interview testimony that Armstrong has herself been aware for a long time of the importance of costume design in her films. Interview commentary from Armstrong about costuming in *Little Women* is illustrative of this. She states: 'I remember with Winona on *Little Women*, there we were, everybody's rehearsing in T-shirts and heavy jeans and baggy pants and so on. But when she put on one of Jo's dresses, and the wig, she went, "Oh, I've got it." At that time too she had a real short tomboy cut, so the hair was also part of it ... I also remember when I did a film called *The Last Days of Chez Nous* in Australia, with Bill Hunter – who's an iconic Australian character actor who always plays big men and strong, fighting men. I was casting him to play older than himself, to play the lead character's father, and after he was with Janet in wardrobe fittings he had these old-man shorts on and knee-high socks, with these shoes and this pale yellow shirt. He just became an old man right in front of my eyes. By the end of the film, I was treating him like an old man: "Are you OK, Bill? Do you need anything?"' (Ebiri 2016).

Armstrong's understanding of costume's capacity to per-formatively convey meaning in non-verbal ways expresses in practical terms knowledge of costume and fashion that has also been recognised by cultural studies theorists of costume. Stella Bruzzi for example, spells out that clothing possesses an aesthetic discourse and has the capacity to convey meaning in ways that are often independent of body and character (1997: xvi). Bruzzi summarises central questions that have surrounded the role of fashion in cinema, which include (namely) how ex-hibitionist clothes ought to be, whether they should perform a 'spectacular or a subservient role' in film, that is, whether they are largely functional or 'art objects' in their own right (1997: 8). While 'fashion' has had elitist connotations in the past – being identified with only what is extravagant – in film every costume is designed, not only the costly ones. Clothing is a communication device to convey meaning and status, to signal sexuality and employment, and one's position on the social ladder.

Women is finally a most coherent, hermetically sealed, and self-referential cinematic expression, where the movie's central subject would seem to motivate the movie's choice of aesthetic style, which in turn sheds light once again on the central subject.

Conclusion

This chapter has explored the aesthetic presence and affective value of sensual components in three of Gillian Armstrong's films. Sensual components thread through all of Armstrong's films, beyond those discussed here. In this chapter, 'sensual' means connection with the senses: taste, touch, sound, and sight. The cinematic means to create such components is varied, deriving from elements in the *mise-en-scène*, costuming, cinematography, sound design, animation, and the handling of certain themes (like food) in the script. The film selection has been based on the films' respective emphases on these issues and in balance with the appearance of movies in other chapters of this book.

Notes

1   Ben Highmore has made a case that spoken language is already imbued with bodily sense perceptions: humans *fall* in love, are *moved* by tragedy, *shake* with fear (2010).
2   The third source of footage is archival imagery, mostly taken from newspaper clippings, films, or still photographs shot in (or relating to) places where Broadhurst lived and worked, including Shanghai, Burma, London, and Paris from the 1920s, 30s, and 40s.
3   How and to what extent the haptic could be of political value for feminist artistic and cinematic expression has been under-theorised, I believe. Laura Marks clarifies that there is nothing essentially feminine about the haptic but has also called attention to its potential usefulness as a feminist strategy (2002: 7). There is a robust and well-established literature on feminist affect but the literature on feminist media hapticity is not extensive. Anu Koivunen (2015) provides a helpful overview of the long history of feminist film studies' engagement with issues of affect.

5

An ethical cinema: *High Tide* and *The Story of Kerry, Josie and Diana*

Gillian Armstrong's movies are a far cry from the violence-inflected 'extreme' films that have been the focus of many ethical-film investigations. Yet Armstrong has positioned herself as a director with a strong interest in ethics and in films with social worth; at one point she voiced ambitions to become a social worker (Mordue 1989: 270–2). She has claimed a personal ethical working code never to have made a movie she didn't believe in (*High Tide* 1987). Her dramatic features frequently foreground aspects of responsibility, processes of questioning and reflection, characters that are complex and can't be compartmentalised, and a refreshed approach to human encounters; while her documentaries emphasise respect for participants and their well-being, the valuing of experience in her interviewees, and an approach which is participatory and inclusive. Armstrong's interest in ethics is unique and sustained, and she has engaged deeply with it over the course of her long career. What is the evidence that Armstrong is a uniquely ethical filmmaker, and how does her work contribute to our knowledge of feminist film ethics? What ethical standpoint does she bring to her pre-production, production, and post-production? What ethics are textually evident in scripting, cinematography, and/or between characters in the movies she directs?

This chapter divides into two major sections. The first addresses Armstrong's dramatic feature films, and the second addresses her documentaries. Each of the sections reviews relevant philosophical discussions about specific ethical challenges and

opportunities in order to provide context for Armstrong's contributions. Throughout, the chapter highlights how Armstrong
contributes to ethical cinematic discourse by inviting new forms
of audience engagement with real and fictional characters and
by setting a representational model for new ethical relations
between dramatic characters. The films that are discussed and
analysed have been selected for best fit with (and illustration of)
the material and in view of what has been discussed in prior
chapters. Thus movies which form the bases of discussions in
Chapters 2 (*Mrs. Soffel*, *Little Women*, *Charlotte Gray*, and *Death
Defying Acts*), 3 (*My Brilliant Career*, *Oscar and Lucinda*, and *Star
Struck*), and 4 (*The Last Days of Chez Nous*, *Unfolding Florence:
the Many Lives of Florence Broadhurst*, and *Women He's Undressed*)
receive less attention than movies which haven't yet been the
focus of another chapter: *High Tide* and *The Story of Kerry, Josie
and Diana*. In the section of the chapter on documentary, the
focus is on Armstrong's longitudinal multi-part series rather than
Armstrong's portrait documentaries.

Towards a feminist cinematic ethics: beginning with Mulvey

Unlike the field of media ethics, film ethics is a somewhat less
crowded area of scholarship. Film ethical issues range across the
spectrum and include directors' responsibilities to represent
events that may be grave or traumatic, and deliberating the role
that audiences play in consuming these forms of entertainment.
Including phrases like 'Screening the Unwatchable' (Grønstad
2012), 'Foreclosed Encounters' (Downing and Saxton 2010), or
'Haunted Images' (Saxton 2008), scholarship on film and ethics
tends to probe representations at the margins of the socially
acceptable, such as sexual assault (Aaron 2007; Miller 2013;
Grønstad 2012), murder, and even cannibalism. Movies about
such subjects raise thorny questions about directors' responsibilities and financial entanglements and about audiences' pleasure

watching things 'that often represent a gross break with legal or social mores' (Aaron 2007).

The past ten years have seen a mini upsurge in book titles on feminist cinematic ethics. *Feminist Ethics in Film: Reconfiguring Care Through Cinema* (Kupfer 2012); *A Feminine Cinematics: Luce Irigaray, Women and Film* (Bainbridge 2008); *Film and Female Consciousness: Irigaray, Cinema and Thinking Women* (Bolton 2011); *Film and Ethics: Foreclosed Encounters; Towards a Feminist Cinematic Ethics: Claire Denis, Emmanuel Levinas and Jean-Luc Nancy* (Hole 2016) (and some of Teays 2012) are some of the books demonstrating the breadth of feminist engagement.

Feminist interest in ethical cinema is however not new and a comprehensive review would need to go back at least to the mid-1970s, to the best-known and often-quoted feminist essay from this period, Laura Mulvey's 'Visual Pleasure and Narrative Cinema'. Even though the word 'ethics' does not figure anywhere in Mulvey's article, at the heart of it are questions of a profoundly socio-ethical nature concerning how spectatorial enjoyment seems to echo and build upon extra-cinematic networks of power and control, and how mechanisms of objectification dovetail with possibilities for women to seize power, both within and external to narrative cinema. Although some accounts have pronounced feminist film and other 'psycho-semiotic' theories as antithetical to ethical concerns,[1] I am aligned with Downing and Saxton's claim (2010) that ethics has been implicit in many strands of film theory, 'from feminist gaze theory, through postcolonial and queer perspectives, to Zizekian accounts of Hollywood cinema' (2010: 2). In addition to its value for Downing and Saxton, the political potential of Mulvey's work has become a rallying cry for others in important ways. Scott MacKenzie, for example, included the essay in his book about film manifestos and termed it a 'call[s] to arms to change, destroy, and reimagine cinema' (2014: 22–3).[2]

In terms of its relevance for Armstrong, Mulvey's approach is specifically helpful for its foregrounding of the interventionist potential of feminist cinematic practice. While Mulvey is mostly considered a film theorist, the fact that she was also a film practitioner and her remarks aimed as much at filmmakers as at film scholars, has often gone unnoticed (see Gaines 2018: 3; Rich 1998: 73). Mulvey called for change from within cinema itself, and following her, scholars have turned to work by Claire Denis, Jane Campion, Sofia Coppola, Sally Potter, Lynne Ramsay, Susan Streitfeld, Marleen Gorris, and Samira Makhmalbaf in search of blueprints for feminist cinematic ethics.

Like Lisa Downing and Libby Saxton, Kristin Hole, Lucy Bolton, Michele Aaron, Caroline Bainbridge, and others contributing to the growing field of feminist cinematic ethics, I draw a direct line from Mulvey's powerful ideas to films by female directors, including Armstrong, in their potential to devise creative solutions to identified challenges. At the heart of some enquiries is the understanding that cinema is not merely reflective of a social status quo but may provide opportunities for reflecting on one's own moral frame. Michele Aaron provides a useful definition of ethical works as those which may 'nurture reflection, recognition, and responsibility' (Aaron 2007: 109); an ethics of spectatorship, she maintains, demands engagement, implication, and a requirement to reflect, and is opposed to a moral approach.

Armstrong's resolutely anti-didactic stance and resistance to be co-opted into singular political modalities and campaigns, speaks vitally to these qualities and concerns. Ethical dilemmas form the narrative hook and fibre of the stories Armstrong tells, often regardless of genre, setting, and country of production. Armstrong's cinema places characters in challenging situations and forces them to navigate dilemmas of considerable consequence: whether to assist a pair of convicted criminals to escape (*Mrs. Soffel*); how to cut through personal traumas of abandonment and loss to reconnect a mother with a daughter (*High Tide*); how to navigate family relationships in the midst of a major betrayal (*Last Days*); what steps to take after accidentally incriminating another (*Charlotte Gray*); and whether to lie for the ultimate good of providing momentary comfort (*Charlotte Gray*). In each of these movies, conventional understandings of right and wrong, perpetrator and victim, collaborator and traitor, abandoner and abandoned, con-artist and conned, criminal and innocent, are overturned. Roles are often reversed and questioned.

For example, *Mrs. Soffel*, discussed in Chapter 2, uses opening scenes to problematise and upend conventional distinctions between culpable and innocent. The prison warden, Peter Soffel, holds court to mete out a 'sentence' to his children, who are termed 'three little criminals'; shortly after this, the 'dangerous' incarcerated man Ed Biddle winks playfully at Kate Soffel's young son Clarence; the blood of Kate and Ed is confused in their first encounter to reconfigure who is the wounded (the blood on Kate's face is assumed to be hers, but she offers a corrective to the guards: 'No that's his.'). Later, the film offers a strong counter to the idea that Ed and Jack are brutal criminals. When the Stevenson family, who feed Ed, Jack, and Kate, learn their true identities, Mrs Stevenson snatches a kitten (which Jack has been cuddling) from his hands; to audiences this appears both comic and absurd given Jack's obvious tenderness with the animal. After their identities are discovered and they move to leave the Stevenson home, Kate ineptly shoots the pistol into the air. As the older townspeople huddle in fear, Ed (smiling broadly) cries sarcastically 'See that? You better stand back! We're two desperate fugitives and she's ruthless and insane.' Category confusion such as this within a film whose themes are clearly anti-death penalty seems reflexive and designed, as Vincent Bohlinger has claimed, to elicit contemplation in the viewer (Bohlinger 2014: 127).

Armstrong's small-budget, Australian-shot, contemporary-set movie *The Last Days of Chez Nous*, discussed in Chapter 4, tells what happens when a married man falls in love with a woman who also happens to be his wife's sister. Much of the critical praise for the movie noted its unclichéd (Ebert 1993) refusal to demonise either woman (Travers 1993) and willingness to stage the sisters' relationship as equally (if not more) important than either sister's relationship to the central male character (Caputo 1992: 7; Béar 1993). Where commercial cinema is replete with examples of the demonic 'other woman' and long-suffering jilted wives, no such pat characterisation is on offer here. *Last Days* forwards a complex portrayal of women characters beyond the normative, conventional 'strong female character' (Worthy 2017). Looked at together, both *Last Days* and *Mrs. Soffel* revisit and reinvent culturally despised categories to create more nuanced portraits.

As ought to be evident from the above discussion, Armstrong's ethical innovations become especially clear in her reflexive, novel, and oftentimes ambiguous construction of characters in ways that overtly rewrite and depart Hollywood norms while resolutely remaining inside popular conventions. As discussed in Chapters 2 and 3, many of Armstrong's domestic and international feature films revise popular forms in important and complex ways; their rewriting of movie characters as more ambiguous and potentially more inscrutable both puts pressure on conventional forms and stories and lays the path for reflexive ethical engagement in audiences.

High Tide (1987)

Armstrong's third Australian-shot feature film *High Tide* includes characters that are multifaceted, interesting, engaging, and in direct dialogue with characters found in established commercial forms. As Armstrong's first feature-length drama set in the present-day, *High Tide* tracks the thorny reunion of a mother with a daughter whom she abandoned at birth; central to it are moments of potentially high drama, including the revelation of past secrets, recollections of the abandonment, and not least the discovery of the biological relationship itself. On the face of it, *High Tide* revisits popular story themes from American maternal melodrama cycles of the 1930s and 40s, such as *Stella Dallas* (1937), *Mildred Pierce* (1945), and the racially themed *Imitation of Life* (1934; 1959). But in formal terms, the rhetorics of the film and the precise playing out of the narrative have little to do with popular melodrama. The film is shot in a realist style, with mostly diegetic or atmospheric music; its ending involves a tentative recommitment of Ally and Lilli to each other, rather than their separation. Most significantly,

High Tide avoids themes of melodramatic sacrifice and suffering. Yet even without recourse to such modalities, *High Tide* remains intensely affecting.

At the centre of the story is adult Lilli (played by Judy Davis), a freewheeling backup singer who performs in the band of an Elvis impersonator, and daughter Ally (played by newcomer Claudia Karvan). The opening few moments emphasise their differences and thus intimate the improbability of their becoming friends. Right after the credit sequence, Lester, the Elvis impersonator, bursts on to the screen, swaggering and strutting around a stage, while Lilli shimmies, dances, and sings in sync with two other singers. Memorably, the singers wear sheer white wigs and fishtailed, sequined, shimmery dresses. The music fades down and the camera speeds across a richly coloured, bright brown, shiny seaside landscape (captured by cinematographer Russell Boyd) before coming to rest on Ally, wearing a wetsuit, with arms outstretched, floating gently in a shallow rock pool in the bright light of day. The light catches around Ally's neck and the ensuing shot shows a close-up of the side of Ally's face, half-immersed in the water. Where Lilli is associated with artifice, Ally is situated in nature. Where Lilli performs in the night-time, Ally is depicted in broad daylight.

Shortly after this introductory sequence, Ally spies Lilli in the pub performing. Now a teenager, Ally has outgrown the restrictive parenting style of her paternal grandmother and guardian Bet (Jan Adele) and is inexplicably drawn to the mysterious stranger, without knowing who the stranger is. A second encounter shows Ally on a surfboard, seeing Lilli from afar. Lilli has just been told she is no longer needed on the Elvis tour, and is wandering aimlessly through the sea waves of the beach in Ally's town, clearly out of place against the bright beach backdrop, in her very dark lipstick and long, dark coat. Atmospheric music plays on the soundtrack and the takes of her are long in duration and clearly uneconomical from a commercial cinema point of view. A subsequent scene taking place later that night shows Ally supporting a clearly inebriated Lilli to move towards the direction of her caravan. The roles are reversed, in that daughter is caring for mother, and the scene is shot completely devoid of judgement, as Ally helps Lilli gain shelter for the night.

In her writing about *High Tide*, Felicity Collins claims the task of the film is to transform the space of maternal abandon via new ways of seeing (1999: 46). For this to occur, the aptly termed town of Eden (where Ally and Lilli meet) must be refigured and cinematographically reframed to allow space for new relations (Collins 1999: 50). Remaking the generic space of commercial cinema is furthermore central to this task. While a maternal melodrama would exploit the process of Ally's and Lilli's learning of each other's identities for dramatic potential and/or the mutual discovery as an 'aha' moment, *High Tide* permits the story to unfold in a way that is devoid of predictable or easily legible emotionalism. It is worth exploring in some detail how this all-important relationship is revealed to various characters over the movie's course.

Bet and Lilli come to learn of each other's identity before anyone else in the film. The shot of Bet's face as she enters the laundromat and spies Lilli for the first time is held for just one beat longer than audiences expect; it is a medium (not a close-up) shot with little camera movement, and there is no music whatsoever to add build up to the encounter. The shot of Davis's face, in this scene, after Bet and Ally depart, is crafted with a similar spare subtlety, depicting Lilli only slightly closer to the camera than Bet in the prior shot, taking a few rapid breaths. When Bet goes to Lilli's caravan in the subsequent scene, there is expressive language, but importantly it issues not from Lilli but from the supporting character, Bet. As Bet confronts Lilli, she ventures loudly and with anger, 'Well, I don't want her knowing!', 'You've come to get her', and 'You've done enough damage . . . if you breathe one word I'll kill you!' Significantly, Lilli's remains the voice of calm, as she answers quietly, 'Look I didn't know you were here.'

The next character who learns of the relationship is Lilli's boyfriend Mick (Colin Friels). Lilli directly informs him that Ally is her daughter, yet as in the scene between Lilli and Bet, Lilli's emotions are again restrained. She delivers the information to him in a matter-of-fact manner, staring out the window, with her back to him. A little while later, when Ally finally comes to understand that Lilli is her mother, she learns this indirectly, through Mick, who encounters her in the public space of the newsagent's shop, where the possibilities for the emotional outburst or tears are muted. Mick enquires whether Lilli said 'anything' to Ally, and Ally responds that she doesn't know what Mick is talking about. The scene plays out in a series of shot-reverse-shots, until Mick finally says quietly and directly, 'She's your mum.' Wordless, Ally runs from the shop to Lilli's caravan and to the beach, where a still camera on Ally's face as she pauses before running across the sand gives audiences time to contemplate what Ally may be feeling, but without confirmation. Even when Ally finally accosts Lilli on the beach, the emotion on her face is controlled. When Lilli finally tries to tell Ally her story, the explanation comes across as authentic and complex; Lilli explains how when Ally's father died, she felt angry, useless, and incompetent as a mother and essentially prevented herself from continuing to love her own daughter. The sentiments Lilli describes seem contradictory and are not fully adequate to explain what has transpired. Confused, Ally keeps pressing Lilli to clarify, revealing the difficulty of comprehending how a mother could 'give away' her own daughter and the simultaneous importance of embracing the discomfort that comes from that not-knowing.

The value of ambiguity in fiction and its ability to stimulate ethical thinking has been noted by a number of philosophers, from Simone de Beauvoir and Maurice Merleau-Ponty to Emmanuel Levinas. While Levinas did not commit himself to the study of aesthetics, his ideas have been espoused within several studies of cinema, where, in the words of Kristin Hole, he teaches us to value what may not yet be known, to resist the 'lure of full comprehension, to let things lie in the darker spaces, to value ungraspable movement, and to be open to the encounter with what we cannot know' (1989: 87). In film studies, the valuing of formally ambiguous cinematic representation has frequently been yoked to the valorising of 'challenging' modernist and/or avant-garde works rather than realist forms; avant-garde and/or modernist films have received praise for their ability to make audiences think and for the distanced and sometimes disoriented modes of engagement they elicit.

Evaluations of characters who, like Lilli, are realist within the terms of their narratives, but who are ambiguous, messy, and flawed – in possession of a heightened capacity for mistake-making and/or also inscrutable at times – are less prevalent in the discipline of film studies. Research on the value of flawed and ambiguous characters in popular media can be found in the disciplines of psychology and moral philosophy (see Eden et al. 2017; Krakowiak and Oliver 2012; Taylor 2011; Akass and McCabe 2011). A helpful explanation of the value of such characters comes from moral philosopher Craig Taylor (2011), who highlights the potential for ambiguous characters to create critical self-awareness in readers. In an essay about the literary classic *Lord Jim*, Taylor analyses responses to Jim's character as evidence of the discomfort readers may have with Jim's shameful act of abandoning eight hundred pilgrims as his ship was sinking. Taylor urges readers to resist rationalising such characters and underscores the heuristic value of ambiguously constructed characters to 'bring home the gaps that inevitably exist for us in that moral sensibility' (2011: 87).

Kim Akass and Janet McCabe assert the value of ambiguity in popular media characters from a feminist perspective (2011).[3] Akass and McCabe describe their reaction to Carmela Soprano, the lead woman character and mafia boss's wife from the popular serial television drama *The Sopranos*, as 'hesitancy, confusion, hand wringing, and contradiction' (2011: 94). Their long-standing interest in Carmela and other 'Sopranos women' revolves around how such characters manage to carve out 'narrative power and influence from the most unpromising and uncompromising of situations' (2011: 94). While Taylor and Akass and McCabe are writing about different forms than Armstrong's (literature in Taylor's case and television in Akass and McCabe's), these ideas resonate with many aspects of Armstrong's cinema, where ambiguity, messiness, and inscrutability are central components of characters and celebrated within Armstrong's stories.

In her Australian-shot movies especially, the freedom Armstrong typically enjoyed working closely with writers and producers ensured an ability to create complex protagonists with the above-named capacities. Characters within her dramatic features are never black and white heroes or villains and may possess motivations that appear complex in ways I have outlined. While Armstrong's larger-budget overseas-financed period features have not tended to allow as much flexibility (or directorial input) in pre-production, Armstrong has always maintained that she selected projects on account of feeling passionate about them; and complexity of character appears to have been an important key to Armstrong's ability to attach to a script.

The UK hybrid comedy-period movie *Death Defying Acts* includes leading characters – in this case, a mother-daughter fortune-telling team – with moral values that are protean and difficult to decipher. As mentioned in Chapter 2, Mary McGarvie is a fraudulent vaudeville psychic who preys on vulnerable audience members by pretending to summon their dead relatives, and who directs her eleven-year-old daughter Benji to assist in the con. When Mary encounters Harry Houdini, the deceit is ultimately exposed, but by a twist of circumstances at the movie's end, Benji does seem to make contact with Houdini's dead mother and thus overturns her prior construction as a fake. The film thus thwarts audience expectations about the female protagonists and goes one step further: it centres the narrative twist upon their ability to confound conventional divisions between authentic and fake, liar and truth-teller.

In *Charlotte Gray*, we find a similar dynamic at work. As previously described, the movie tells the story of a Scotswoman who is recruited into British Special Operations and offered a chance to parachute behind enemy lines into France in World War Two in search of her captured RAF lover. Centring on the actions of a woman spy in wartime, *Charlotte Gray* reflexively sows uncertainty about its lead character's political allegiance from the very beginning of the story. 'How could we have known that war never trades in such certainties? For where nothing is unthinkable, anything could be true. Even a lie', offers Charlotte's voice-over at the movie's opening. In a departure from the bestselling novel by Sebastian Faulks on which the movie was based, Charlotte's allegiance to the cause of French communism is cast as ambiguous at several points in the movie. She dreams up plans to advance the cause but when some communist friends are killed, Charlotte's responsibility for these deaths comes into question. Although she denies any role in the killings, in a subsequent scene the unsettling idea is introduced that the killing of the communists could have been an Allied plot in which Charlotte played an unwitting part. Self-doubt and questioning are integral to Charlotte's identity. When an operative with whom she has shared a personal moment is suddenly seized by Vichy police, the camera's lingering on Cate Blanchett highlights the character's own thought process about what role she might unwittingly have played in the process, and whether approaching the police might possibly help the other operative. At the end of the film, Charlotte asserts herself by writing a pseudonymous letter to two Jewish boys in hopes of providing comfort. There is an irony that this decisive contribution itself comprises an act of falsehood – pretending to be someone she is not.

While some reviewers criticised the movie's incorporation of romance themes as implausible, most of the positive assessments of the movie cycled back to Blanchett's character, which received praise for its complexity (Ebert 2002; Errigo 2000; Holden 2001). In Armstrong's adaptation, Charlotte's indecipherability is not just incidental to the plot, it is a key theme around which the plot revolves. Through these approaches and mechanisms, Armstrong requires audiences to exert effort to understand character motivation, lends value to ambiguity, and centres and celebrates it as a key narrative lynchpin.

Opportunities for empathy

In addition to providing opportunities for category confusion and character ambiguity, Armstrong's movies provide means for empathetic engagement with characters. The value of empathy and its materialisation in film have been subjects of growing interest in the twenty-first century, with interdisciplinary explorations of cinematic empathy now carried out across the fields of film theory, philosophy of ethics, and aesthetics; scholars have canvassed cinema for its ability to foster empathetic and embodied responses (Sinnerbrink 2016: 82). Through clever deployment of a range of rhetorical devices including point-of-view shots, voice-over narration, subjective imagery, and close-ups, movies may produce what Robert Sinnerbrink terms 'cinempathy': the offering of 'experientially rich, context-sensitive', multi-perspectival understandings (Sinnerbrink 2016: 80).

Armstrong's movies do this via a range of devices and movie themes. In the scene when Kate Soffel first encounters the convicted criminal Ed Biddle, a brief initial shot featuring Ed's and Kate's respective faces in frame, gives way to a series of alternating shot-reverse shots of their respective faces obscured by prison bars. There is a stylised use of darkness and shadow so that Ed's face appears vertically bisected by the prison bars and one half is obscured in darkness. Kate is shot from Ed's point of view, also through prison bars, so that her face also appears cut by wide vertical black stripes. Both faces are expressive and hold an uninterrupted gaze at the other person, which does not completely coincide with the dialogue that is being spoken. For example, partly through the scene, Ed calls out to his brother, without breaking his stare at Kate. Throughout, the faces of the two protagonists are intense and focused and there is little camera movement, contrasting sharply with what has previously been a chaotic-appearing scene.

In emotional and phenomenological terms, the function of this sequence is twofold: on the one hand, via the images of the mutually intense gazes, the sequence clearly suggests the growing empathy Kate Soffel and Ed Biddle are beginning to feel for each other. On the other hand, the scene is highly likely to elicit those very same feelings for the two characters, from audiences. Phenomenological interpretations define empathy as an 'other-oriented emotional process that involves a form of emotional imagination, understood as "feeling with" a person or a protagonist in a way that "depends on our imagining what [that person's] beliefs, desires, and so on might be"' (Stadler 2014: 30).[4] Aesthetically, the sequence contains the markers that Carl Plantinga has identified within 'scenes of empathy' – a focus on expressive facial features, the use of minimal camera movement to permit the perception of expression, somewhat longer takes, the selective use of shadow and darkness, and, importantly, close-ups (Plantinga 1999: 239–55).[5]

The important rhetorical device here is the close-up. In her outlining of the history of the cinematic close-up in early twentieth-century writings about cinema, Mary Ann Doane notes how the close-up was considered a privileged cinematic device and presumed to provide a direct 'vertical gateway' to the image as a whole. While the close-up showed only a portion of an actor's body, its value was often elevated beyond that of the entire body (Doane 2003). In the writings of Walter Benjamin and others, the close-up was said to offer a more intimate, immediate, and manageable contemplation than what would typically be on offer within the narrative overall, aimed directly at audiences and able to circumvent narrative scripting.

Let me return to *High Tide* to consider how this might operate. In this movie, the close-up is the rhetorical device which is used to introduce characters (Ally relaxing in a tidal pool; Lilli drag racing against the Elvis impersonator, Lester), to attract audience's attention to certain characters, and to suggest building or changing relationships between characters. Facial close-ups express in wordless ways emotion felt by one character towards another. For example, before Lilli and Ally have a chance to meet, Ally spies Lilli in a pub; the film cross-cuts between close-ups of Lilli's face (unaware) and Ally's brightly lit face looking at Lilli, suggesting a pending connection in advance of their actual meeting. The scene of Ally and Lilli's subsequent meeting in the caravan bathroom begins with a close-up of Ally's fingers, touching the water coming from the shower head; nearly fifteen seconds in duration, the shot includes a pan down and across from the shower head to Ally's face, dripping with water. In this sequence, Lilli is now seen observing her daughter in the shower, as the camera adopts her point of view to show the shaving of Ally's calf.

Organised around alternating facial close-ups, scenes like these of Ally observing Lilli (and Lilli observing Ally) are the grammar through which the growing relationship is indicated and progressed. Intimate and wordless, shots and sequences such as these emphasise the unique capacities of film as a visual medium and furthermore indicate practices of *noticing* on Lilli's (and Ally's) part, as Lilli's personal way of engaging with the world and specifically coming to know the daughter she hasn't seen for many years. Because of the slowness of these scenes and how the camera lingers, audiences are encouraged to take up Lilli's quietly observant stance and to take note how the light falls across Ally's face and the patterns made by the razor (for example). As the relationships progress, changes and developments continue to be marked by close-ups: Ally and Lilli in the café where they first go after meeting; Ally's confronting Lilli and demanding to be told about the past; and finally Lilli's invitation to Ally to leave Bet and join her. In a movie that emphasises (as described) processes of not knowing and uncertainty, the faces offer the fullest information available.

The subject of the face in cinema has a long critical history. In the early part of the twentieth century when cinema was in its infancy, Bela Balazs and Jean Epstein posited that the facial close-up promised a transparency and lack of mediation (Doane 2003: 120). Common to both Balazs and Epstein is an understanding that facial close-ups are privileged sites of individuation (i.e. the person's uniqueness is embodied in their face) and the 'primary tool of intersubjectivity, of relation to or communication with the other' (Doane 2003: 95).[6] Through close-ups, understanding is communicated, empathy is generated, and a means of approach to other people is demonstrated.

The key word here is 'other': in Armstrong's cinema, close-ups assist in both managing and manipulating ethical encounters between characters whose relationship has yet to unfold (such as

Ally and Lilli) and between characters who are 'other' (marked by their alterity) to each other, in terms (typically) of their gender or socio-economic background. It has been noted that Armstrong's cinema is somewhat out of step with current day women's filmmaking and scholarship with its emphasis on pluralism and the politics of race (Smaill 2011: 107); Armstrong's cinema overall is not racially diverse and racial alterity is not often thematised in Armstrong's work.

Armstrong's cinema does display a consistent interest in working-class experience and her movies have frequently included themes of aspiration, cross-class (im)mobilities, working-class austerity, and cross-class couples. The thematising of class in her movies is varied: while in *My Brilliant Career*, class difference appears as an impediment to the central relationship (Sybylla fears losing her identity through marriage to the more well-to-do Harry), other movies feature characters who seek relationships with people from different classes and who appear drawn to difference and alterity: a prison warden's wife and a convicted criminal (in *Mrs. Soffel*); Oscar Hopkins, from a modest English background, and the Australian aristocrat Lucinda Leplastrier (in *Oscar and Lucinda*); the Scotswoman Charlotte Gray and the Jewish Frenchman Julien Levade (*Charlotte Gray*).

I believe it is worth emphasising these components of difference, both because of their significance for Armstrong's cinema and because they have often been overlooked in the critical literature on Armstrong. The philosopher who is most closely identified with issues of alterity and otherness is Lithuanian-born Emmanuel Levinas. While a thorough discussion of this major philosopher's work is outside the scope of this book, it is worth pointing out that Levinas's work has been adopted in a number of works on feminism and on cinema (including works about feminist cinema) and his understanding of and approach to alterity may help shed light, I believe, on Armstrong's innovations in this regard.

It is easy to map Levinas's philosophical findings on to his own personal experience as a Jewish man living in occupied France.

Levinas became a French citizen and was drafted in 1939; after the war he worked for the Alliance Israélite Universelle in Paris, an organisation which aimed to emancipate Jews in countries where they could not obtain citizenship (Chanter 2001: 7). Author of the major philosophical works *Totality and Infinity* (1961) and *Otherwise than Being or Beyond Essence* (1974), Levinas is sometimes referred to as the founder of modern ethics where he is credited with subverting the relationship between ethics and philosophy. Where philosophy had occupied itself with questions of being (ontology), Levinas posited a primacy of ethics that would be arrived at via encounters with others and the notion that it wasn't possible to approach questions of ontology without first approaching the question of alterity. Alterity, he maintained, was the primary and most important experience. Levinas called this experience coming face to face with the Other and advanced a thesis that the face of the Other both 'commands' a person and goes beyond being, is infinite (Chanter 2001: 7).

For Levinas, the 'Other' is unknowable, absolute, and unable to be assimilated or subordinated into an object. As Therese Davis explains:

> becoming 'I' involves first facing up to responsibility for the Other: 'Responsibility for the Other, for the naked face of the first individual to come along, a responsibility that goes beyond what I may or may not have done to the Other, whatever act I may or may not have committed, as if I were devoted to the other before being devoted to myself.' (Davis 2004: 11)[7]

From Levinas we get a new 'framework' for dealing with differences (Adital and Strier 2010).

While Levinas's comprehension of alterity and its relation to being has value, his response to aesthetics notoriously bordered on the hostile, and he offers little help in imagining what an application of his ideas within a cinematic realm might look like. Kristin Hole's work is especially useful in exemplifying what a cinematic application of Levinas would look like and indeed how to recognise the rhetoric of alterity. Hole elevates the concept of the face-to-face encounter as the 'definitive image' of Levinas's ethics; and she maintains that a radical alterity in filmmaking 'requires an other brought close enough that their contours are not so easily discernible' (2016: 89). Hole reminds us of the centrality of the figure of the 'stranger' in Levinas's conception, and suggests that an encounter with alterity might include cinema tropes such as the containing of two characters within a single frame (2016: 95), a suggestion of character interrelatedness that is not entirely spelled out (2016: 95), encounters between characters that appear to take place apart from the normative time-space continuum of the movie narrative (2016: 96), intrusions of others which are disruptive (2016: 99), and the option not to psychologise characters and to maintain otherness.

In spite of Armstrong's reputation for creating stories about strong women, in many of her movies Armstrong assigns equitable screen time, dialogue, and agency to both members of the respective heterosexual couple. Many of her dramatic features incorporate two or more perspectives to create a co-telling of the story (*Starstruck*; *Mrs. Soffel*; *High Tide*; *Last Days*; *Little Women*; *Oscar and Lucinda*; *Death Defying Acts*); some of her movies expressly draw attention to this co-telling via the employment of a voice-over from a neutral third party, who is not part of the main heterosexual couple (i.e. the grandchild in *Oscar and Lucinda*; the daughter in *Death Defying Acts*). The effect of these strategies is that narrative screen time is distributed across more than a single character, stories are told from multiple points of view, and agency is shared and distributed.

Across the history of cinema there are ample examples of approaches which approximate what Armstrong accomplishes; these would include films from all periods of Hollywood cinema which tell stories from more than one point of view (ranging from *Grand Hotel* (1932) to *Citizen Kane* (1941) to *Psycho* (1960)) and films that employ multi-perspectival storytelling in order to undermine narrational authority (whose examples would include everything from *Thin Blue Line* (1988), to *Rashamon* (1950), to *Courage Under Fire* (1996)).

What distinguishes Armstrong's efforts is not the distribution of the storytelling per se, but the recurring gendering of these strategies, that is, the fact that the narration tends to be distributed amongst women characters or amongst a woman and a man character. Women are frequently positioned at the centre of Armstrong's stories or may share the storytelling with male friends or lovers, but they are always positioned as authoritative and never positioned as 'supporting'. The effect of this approach is subtle but wide-ranging in its effect on voice and agency, noted at the start of the chapter: both women and men are desiring beings, subjects and objects in equal measure, and problem-solvers, irrespective of gender. In so doing, Armstrong provides a new approach to heterosexual relationships and relationships across social classes.

In addition to providing opportunities for new and equitable relationships within heterosexual couples, Armstrong provides a further innovation in her depiction of communities of women. Informed by feminist philosophy (in particular the ideas of French philosopher Luce Irigaray), a new generation of film theorists have bemoaned the tendency of commercial cinema to polarise women into opposing binary oppositions and/or to include not more than one lead female character within popular narratives; these precepts have in turn been picked up and promoted via popular metrics like the Bechdel test. The Bechdel test assigns positive 'ticks' on account of a movie's inclusion of at least two major female characters who talk to each other about subjects other than men. The test offers a tracking mechanism for pop culture forms that improve on stereo-typical and limiting gender representations.

Well before the introduction of the Bechdel test and, to my knowledge, without having read any of the above-named philosophy, Armstrong's cinema was demonstrating interest in and making space for unique and unusual female characters and highly complex groups of women, all of which would clearly pass the test and serve as alternative models to the representational issues noted by feminist philosophers like Luce Irigaray. *High Tide, The Last Days of Chez Nous, Little Women, Death Defying Acts*, as well as nearly all of Armstrong's documentaries are populated by communities and indeed generations of women characters, as outlined in this book's introduction. To continue to explore Armstrong's interest, I'd like now to consider Armstrong's five-part longitudinal documentary series, *The Story of Kerry, Josie and Diana.*

Armstrong's documentary ethics

Ethical considerations have been integral to documentary production since at least 1922 when what has been called the world's first documentary initially screened. When Robert Flaherty asked the Inuit actors he was working with to imperil themselves hunting a walrus with weapons that were no longer part of their hunting arsenal in *Nanook of the North*, he entered the domain of documentary ethics: the obligation filmmakers have to 'actual people whose lives spill beyond the frame' (Nichols 2016: 155). With few exceptions, all documentary engages with the real world and with real people (whether living or dead), and many documentaries use images with some degree of indexicality. Many include images of actual people sharing stories from their own lives and experiences, even if their descriptions are subjective, stretches of the truth, or contain errors. There are many caveats cautioning us against equating documentary simply and unwaveringly with the real, but there is no doubt that more is at stake when social actors are invited to share portions of their lives in a documentary than when professional actors are invited to act in a fiction film.

Many professional bodies are governed by codes (e.g. law, journalism, medicine, etc.) but documentary is not one of them; there is no formal code of ethics for documentary practitioners. Nonetheless all documentary practitioners are expected to conform to certain professional standards. When documentaries engage social actors from the real world, documentary practitioners are expected not to harm them and to bear their welfare in mind throughout the production processes. The history of documentary production is rife with charges of ethical misbehaviour, including not respecting or outright mistreating documentary participants, lying or stretching of the truth beyond what is acceptable, and/or presenting the facts in a way that is deemed offensive or overly simplistic. For example, Dennis O'Rourke was condemned for including scenes of an underage participant telling potentially incriminating stories in *Cunnamulla* (Kelly 2011) and *KONY 2012* was criticised for forwarding a naïve, ill-informed, white-centric approach to the complex problem of child soldiers in central Africa (Hershey and Artime 2014). In the history of documentary practice there are also countless examples of praiseworthy approaches, both historical and contemporary; most of these identify cases where participants are given voice and agency within specific documentaries. Thus French filmmaker Jean Rouch has received praise for his early participatory, polyvocal approach in the ethno-fiction *Jaguar*, which invited collaborative input (in the form of running commentary) from the participants (Nannicelli 2006).

In addition to being the director of a sizable body of fictional work, Gillian Armstrong has a well-established reputation as the creator of popular, highly regarded, formally significant documentaries. Her documentary features comprise two major types: aesthetically stylised portraits (on the one hand) and a multi-part, longitudinal series about three working-class women in South Australia (on the other). As discussed in Chapter 4, *Women He's Undressed* and *Unfolding Florence: The Many Lives of Florence Broadhurst* portray two important figures in the arts community and seek answers about their respective subjects' lives, both of whom are long deceased. *The Story of Kerry, Josie and Diana* (1976–2009) was commissioned by the South Australian Film Corporation, shot over a time span of thirty-four years, and comprises five works: *Smokes and Lollies* (1976), *Fourteen's Good, Eighteen's Better* (1980), *Bingo, Bridesmaids and Braces* (1988), *Not Fourteen Again* (1996), and *Love, Lust & Lies* (2010). The series uses mostly observational and interview footage of three girls (then women) whom Armstrong first met at an Adelaide youth centre when she journeyed to South Australia explicitly to make a film about working-class girls.

The ethical challenges documentary filmmakers face typically differ from film to film and participant to participant, and Armstrong's movies are no exception in this regard. Documentaries about people in the public domain – like politicians or rock stars or costume designers – will obviously prompt different ethical approaches than documentaries about private citizens. Documentaries about living participants compel different negotiations than documentaries about people who are deceased. The trust required by longitudinal documentaries is theoretically greater than what a non-longitudinal documentary requires, in that if participants are unhappy with the outcome of one film in a series, they obviously can decline future invitations to participate in subsequent projects, and the series will essentially terminate. A director's stakes in protecting participant privacy and in creating a movie that participants will respond favourably to, is obviously higher than with non-longitudinal works. At the same time, documentaries that are flattering to the exclusion of all other qualities are not going to yield the critical accolades or audience responses that directors seek.

As a longitudinal series about what eventually became three multi-generational working-class families in the private domain, *The Story of Kerry, Josie and Diana* required a recurring set of negotiations over a long period of time with a large and expanding cast of social actors that is exceptional and sets the series apart from Armstrong's other documentaries and indeed most other documentaries in general. For these reasons, the remainder of the chapter brings focus to the series.

Participant well-being

There are numerous ways to assess the ethics of documentary production. Evidence may be available in the form of production records, interviews, and other archival materials. Ethics may be gleaned in the use to which a documentary is put after release.

For example, the production company Brave New Films employs a 'coalition model' to produce and screen movies for the express purpose of generating activist activities; BNF are known less for their aesthetic achievements than for their abilities to make contributions in grassroots activist spheres (Christiensen 2009).

A quick glance at interview testimony with Armstrong paints a portrait of a director with a sustained concern for the well-being of her participants. At numerous times Armstrong has alluded to the fact that the three Adelaide girls (and their respective families) were at the forefront of the director's mind:

> 'The thing that's hardest for me now … is the fact of it getting any publicity. I worry about journalists writing about the film. And that the women will read it. I hope people are sensitive enough when they write to realise that these are real people.' (Mordue 1989: 271)

In questions about the series over the years, Armstrong deflects queries about a current or future film iteration with phrases like 'it depends on the three women …' Armstrong has recurringly voiced concern that one of the women would read reviews of movies in which they appeared and be negatively affected.

In terms of documentary histories and forms, Armstrong's series has been compared on numerous occasions with the British *Seven Up* series in spite of clear differences between the two works. The British series was designed as a social analysis to highlight the salient differences of class on outcome; Armstrong's began as an exploration of the lives of three girls from the same working-class background. *Seven Up* was conceived as a multi-part series from the start, where *Smokes and Lollies*, the first iteration, was conceived as a stand-alone documentary that was only decided to be built on after *Smokes and Lollies* was released. Finally, the formal construction of the *Seven Up* movies is the question and answer format. Armstrong's movies include both interview footage, often shot in the women's home environments, and observational footage shot while the women are preparing dinner, getting their children ready for school, or talking with family members. From the very start the series required a unique level of trust between Armstrong and her participants.

As a series about women's lives, the series obviously parallels Armstrong's own life and touches on elements about which she has personal passion. As the women have aged, so Armstrong has aged; these processes are noted openly in the movie. Armstrong has spoken freely about how she acted as a mentor at times, providing advice to the girls on matters of family planning and so on.

As for the movies' wider potential, there is evidence Armstrong has on occasion leveraged her success with the series to advocate for certain issues or to increase public awareness of political causes. The second movie in the series, *Fourteen's Good, Eighteen's Better*, won an award from the Victorian Teachers' Federation and has often been used in schools (Mordue 1989). Armstrong has spoken about the film's advocacy potential when she met with politicians Susan Ryan and Bill Hayden around this same period (1980) (Hall 2017).[8]

Axiographics

In addition to the above means, the actual text of the documentary can also provide insight into a documentary's ethics. Bill Nichols uses the term 'axiographics' to identify the inscription of documentary ethics onto the text of a movie, in Nichols's words 'the question of how values, particularly an ethics of representation, comes to be known and experienced in relation to space' (1992: 77). Determining axiographics may open understanding on to the documentary filmmaker's stance regarding the social reality they are trying to represent and may provide a means of assessing a director's position vis-à-vis the world they are putting on screen. Documentary ethics have a material impact on how social actors should (and should not) be treated, what stories can (or cannot) be told, what contents can (or cannot) be included. The outcome of these negotiations is apparent in the film that is finally produced. These negotiations do not result in black and white solutions and each outcome must be negotiated in varying stages of production, between directors and participants, and/or between directors and producers and participants, and/or with editors in post-production.

Documentary has long wrestled with questions of voice and knowledge in their relations to power, and analysts of documentary have long asked: 'With which participant's/participants' voice(s) does the documentary align?'; 'Who is the expert and holds the key to knowledge, filmmaker or participant?'; 'What roles do documentary filmmaker and documentary interviewee play?' The history of documentary contains numerous examples of directors aiming for a more participatory or inclusive approach and ways to make visible circuits and economies of labour that previously were obscured. Grounding such ambitions is the desire to recognise the value of lived experience and to prioritise it over and above scientific knowledge typically meted out by outsiders. Ultimately, many filmmakers seek to return to the subjects of their documentaries a modicum of self-determination and power, which begins with their being recognised as experts of their own experiences. As Faye Ginsberg states, '[T]his effort to turn the tables on the historical trajectory of the power relations embedded in research monographs, photography, and ethnographic practice is intentional' (Ginsberg 2002: 55).

In interviews about the documentaries, Armstrong has often sought to narrow the gap between herself and her actors, claiming (for example) how at the first meeting the girls mistook her for another girl at the youth centre (Shirley 2011). While Armstrong has noted the age difference and spoken in interviews about being able to provide advice to the girls on occasion, within the body of her movies Armstrong is more likely to place herself on the same representational plane as her participants. In later movies especially, Armstrong is typically seen being greeted at the door like an old friend when she arrives at the respective women's houses. The impression of familiarity between Armstrong and Josie, Kerry, and Diana is conveyed, and Armstrong cannot then be cast as expert.

Towards the end of the fourth movie in the series (which scene is repeated in the fifth movie), questions that Armstrong asked of each woman are turned on to her: Josie turns to ask the director the same question she has just been asked, 'What would *you* like to be doing in the next ten years?' In the final scene of *Love, Lust, and Lies* Armstrong is shown sitting with the three women on the beach, drinking sparkling wine. Such scenes do not of course eradicate the differences between Armstrong (as internationally successful film director) and the three women, nor the power difference between Armstrong (as the movie's director) and the subjects. But they do indicate Armstrong's recognition of the importance of respect between filmmaker and participants.

There is further evidence of respectfulness between Armstrong and the three women. In the fifth and (currently) last instalment of the series, it is revealed that Diana has re-partnered with her old love Fury, while Keith (her partner of episodes 1–4) remains living in the house with the new couple. The relating of this story is perhaps the biggest surprise in the series, and telling it requires respect and skill. Armstrong's approach both recognises the now separate status of the two members of the ex-couple, while also indicating their ongoing togetherness, as family who have lived many years together and their value as co-parents. Armstrong achieves this by conducting separate interviews with Keith and Diana: Keith's interview is shot at a table underneath the carport, while Diana is filmed inside, as she braids Fury's hair. When Armstrong begins asking about Diana's recent reconnection with Fury, she cross-cuts seamlessly between Keith's telling and Diana's. Information from each speaker builds and does not contradict the other as Armstrong cross-cuts, and through editing there is the illusion that Diana and Keith are adding to each other's story, coherently co-telling the story of the break-up, as allies. The two physically separate spaces are woven together to form one seamless space which in turn underscores the impression of harmony between the two. The ultimate result is the respectful conveying of a couple who are technically separated but who remain emotionally unified, and who continue to relate to each other in a harmonious and supportive way. Rather than leveraging the separation and break-up for sensational effect, in these scenes Armstrong parries her own considerable formal skills to create a respectful co-telling of events which both opens new forms of engagement for audiences and produces opportunities for trust between herself and participants.

Armstrong's engagement with scenes of potential drama and heightened emotion in this film is another indicator of her respectful approach. *Love, Lust, and Lies* invites audiences to scrutinise seemingly irrelevant moments – such as an extended squabble about housework – while offering only brief glimpses into deeper issues, such as a character's challenges with health and well-being. Diana describing her fear about having to have surgery for carpal tunnel is one such moment which could invite an exploitative lingering of the camera; Armstrong instead captures Diana's confession of her fear in four brief shots which are edited together via jump cuts. In contrast, a seemingly more 'minor' scene (which follows shortly after) which takes place at Josie's house, about who is doing the washing, is comparably more detailed and lingering, showing the valuing of women's domestic labour and seemingly 'small' events and Armstrong's respectful non-invasive approach to difficult emotions such as Diana's. The outcome is an approach which both respects the privacy of the movie's participants and invites audiences to reconsider which events they deem worthy of scrutiny.

Conclusion

Although Armstrong's fiction films and documentaries have been discussed sequentially, similar themes emerge in each: empathy and respect; the sharing of narrative screen time between multiple male and female characters and characters 'co-telling' of stories; the valuing of ambiguity and inscrutability in characters; and a non-exploitative approach to alterity and otherness (particularly class difference). Documentary rhetoric Armstrong employs demonstrates her commitment not to sensationalise aspects of Josie's, Diana's, or Kerry's life; fiction films also avoid creating moments of sensationalist, heightened drama from emotionally charged moments. Through all of these means, Armstrong creates an innovative and sustained ethical cinema.

Notes

1 Sinnerbrink cast psycho-semiotic theory as antithetical to ethical inquiry: 'These ethical concerns were largely displaced by political and ideological agendas during the 1960s and 70s, a tendency apparent in the rise of Lacanian-Althusserian "psycho-semiotic" and feminist film theory' (2016: 15).
2 MacKenzie qualified how manifestos are linked to the social belief systems that govern how one ought to 'live one's life' (2014: 24); he distinguished between components of a manifesto and simple rules, by claiming that manifestos include an ethical component that 'effect one's morality and ethics in a way that "don't run with scissors" [that is a simple rule] does not' (2014: 24).
3 For further reading on the feminist potential for ambiguity, see Parpart 2010.
4 Stadler is quoting Neill (2006: 252).
5 Plantinga is here summarised in Sinnerbrink (2016: 94).
6 Doane is quoting Deleuze re: 'primary tool of intersubjectivity'.
7 Davis is quoting from Levinas (1989: 83).
8 Armstrong also discusses going to Canberra with *My Brilliant Career* and ending up talking about *Fourteen's Good, Eighteen's Better* (Neill 1988).

Conclusion: a collaborative cinema

Women's involvement in the commercial film industries is varied and diverse. Women comprise an ever-growing group of directors, writers, producers, and other creative practitioners, audience members and fans, critics and journalists, bloggers and academics, many of whom share a goal of augmenting women's power, expression, and voice in and through media, including film. Women's involvement as media creatives and audiences is often informed by long-standing debates in feminism and film studies about representation, power, and pleasure and by newer conversations about representational ethics.

This book has attempted to expand those debates to bring Armstrong into discussion with some of the major approaches to cinema in the post-1990s period. The intention has been to find openings and overlaps where engagement opportunities could be explored. This book has surveyed Armstrong's performance of authorship, her deft responses to genre filmmaking, and the incorporation of ethical and sensual themes in her work. The book's starting point was that Armstrong's films make philosophical and conceptual contributions in and of themselves which in turn contribute to wider theoretical discussions. As media scholars moved squarely into discussions about ethics and affects from the 1990s onwards, and feminist researchers began to re-investigate the value of the popular, Armstrong, it turns out, was ahead of the curve.

In 2016 Armstrong released her most recent movie to date: what has been promoted as the world's biggest crowd-sourced film, *The Inspiring Story of Us*, financed by the Commonwealth Bank of Australia (Carter forthcoming). Receiving footage from all over the country totalling over fifty-five hours in running time, captured on a diversity of equipment and devices including digital cameras, phones, go-pros, and Skype, Armstrong edited the material to form a 23-minute movie in the course of one month ('Gillian Armstrong' 2016).

The Inspiring Story of Us is somewhat of a production anomaly with respect to the other films discussed in this book: while Armstrong edited the materials together, she did not control what was submitted, what was shot, how footage was framed – or camera movement, sound capture, or any other aspects of the production process. *The Inspiring Story of Us* would seem to be a film over which Armstrong exerted less control than usual, but also possibly the most collaborative endeavour of all her films to date.

Or is it? This book has subscribed to an understanding of film authorship where the director is paramount, is scrutinised and receives credit for their creative input over and above the labours of co-creating cinematographers, editors, costume and set designers, producers, and others. On occasion, it has noted Armstrong's relationships with producers and writers and cinematographers on particular projects, but on the whole has said little about the precise contributions of the all-important cadre of professionals – cinematographers, editors, designers, and other creative personnel – with whom Armstrong has worked and on whom her movie-making career truly depends. Chapter 1 noted how Armstrong has worked with many of the same professionals over the course of her films; it is fitting that the book concludes by re-acknowledging the significance of collaboration to her success and Armstrong's own recognition of that. Collaboration is truly the warp and weft of Armstrong's achievements.

Armstrong has spoken highly of her collaborations with producers, writers, and others in movies that include *My Brilliant Career, High Tide, Last Days, Mrs. Soffel*, and many others (Caputo 1992). She has acknowledged the significance of the creative combination of producer, director, and writer and spoken about the intimate relationships she has established with both producers and writers (Caputo 1992: 6). Armstrong's recurring work with Australian industry professionals, such as editor Nicholas Beauman, cinematographers Russell Boyd and Geoffrey Simpson, production designer Luciana Arrighi, and others was noted in Chapter 1 of this book. Armstrong has acknowledged the artistic and personal benefits of working with a continuity of personnel, stating:

> You develop a short-hand of understanding with people you've worked with before. It is efficient, and also you've become friends with them and there's a great sense of support … I know they make me look better … I appreciate the fact that I've got a team who are honest with me; I respect their taste, and I say to young filmmakers, 'Always take the best idea in the room; it's not a matter of your ego but of making great films.' (McFarlane 2008: 21)

Collaboration with women scriptwriters is an especially interesting feature of Armstrong's work, and on at least two occasions (the short film *The Singer and the Dancer* and *High Tide*) resulted in a decision to change the gender of main characters from male to female. Armstrong's activism to increase the profile of women creatives in the screen industries and the power and presence of Australian directors has also not occurred in a vacuum, but in consort with many, many others working in the same political and industrial space.

By drawing attention to the importance of collaboration for Armstrong's activities, accomplishments, and methodologies in the areas of feature film and documentary filmmaking, it is hoped that this book will open up opportunities for further research into the full spectrum of activities that contribute to the making of a 'Gillian Armstrong film'. Through attending to Armstrong's distinct contributions – in feminist cinematic ethics, sensorial cinematic expression, in Australian and international generic forms – this book invites readers to explore and understand all that Armstrong has to offer.

Works cited

Aaron, Michele (2007), *Spectatorship: The Power of Looking On*, New York: Columbia/Wallflower Press.

Adital, Ben-Ari and Roni Strier (2010), 'Rethinking Cultural Competence: What Can We Learn from Levinas?', *The British Journal of Social Work*, 40.7, pp. 2155–67.

Affron, Charles and Mirella Jona Affron (1995), *Sets in Motion: Art Direction and Film Narrative*, London: British Film Institute.

Ahmed, Sara (2014), *The Cultural Politics of Emotion*, Edinburgh: Edinburgh University Press.

Akass, Kim and Janet McCabe (2011), '"Blabbermouth Cunts"; or, Speaking in Tongues: Narrative Crises for Women in *The Sopranos* and Feminist Dilemmas', in David Lavery (ed.), *The Essential Sopranos Reader*, Lexington: University of Kentucky Press, pp. 93–104.

Armstrong, Gillian (1999), 'Little Women: Little by Little', in Raffaele Caputo and Geoff Burton (eds), *Second Take: Australian Film-makers Talk*, Sydney: Allen and Unwin, pp. 102–22.

Arnheim, Rudolph (1957), *Film as Art*, Berkeley: University of California Press.

Atkinson, Sarah and Helen W. Kennedy (2016), 'Introduction – Inside-the-scenes: The rise of experiential cinema', *Participations*, 31.1 (May), pp. 139–51.

Attanasio, Paul (1985), 'Stifling "Soffel"', *The Washington Post*, 9 February, <https://www.washingtonpost.com/archive/lifestyle/1985/02/09/stifling-soffel/e74fa3dc-9f89-4649-b47e-7e572484ad81/?noredirect=on&utm_term=.f8ab400d33ff> (last accessed 22 April 2020).

Avenell, Julia (2006), 'Design for Life: *Unfolding Florence*', *Metro Magazine: Media & Education Magazine*, 150, pp. 68–72.

Badley, Linda, Claire Perkins, and Michele Schreiber (2016), 'Introduction', in Linda Badley, Claire Perkins, and Michele Schreiber (eds), *Indie Reframed:*

Women's Filmmaking and Contemporary American Independent Cinema, Edinburgh: Edinburgh University Press, pp. 1–20.

Bainbridge, Caroline (2008), *A Feminine Cinematics: Luce Irigaray, Women and Film*, Basingstoke: Palgrave Macmillan.

Baker, Candida (1996), 'The Evolution of Gillian Armstrong', *The Age*, 3 August.

Barker, Jennifer (2009), *The Tactile Eye: Touch and the Cinematic Experience*, Berkeley, Los Angeles, and London: University of California Press.

Béar, Liza (1993), 'Gillian Armstrong by Liza Béar', *Bomb Magazine*, 43, 1 April, <https://bombmagazine.org/articles/gillian-armstrong/> (last accessed 22 April 2020).

Behrendt, Larissa (2018), 'The Nightingale review – ambitious, urgent and necessarily brutal. But who is it for?', *The Guardian*, 20 August 2019, <https://www.theguardian.com/film/2019/aug/20/the-nightingale-review-ambitious-urgent-and-necessarily-brutal-but-who-is-it-for> (last accessed 22 April 2020).

Bergfelder, Tim, Sarah Street, and Sue Harris (2007), 'Introduction: Understanding and Interpreting Set Design in Cinema', in Tim Bergfelder, Sarah Street, and Sue Harris (eds), *Film Architecture and the Transnational Imagination: Set Design in 1930s European Cinema*, Amsterdam: Amsterdam University Press, pp. 11–30.

Bohlinger, Vincent (2014), 'Self-reflexivity and historical revision in *A Moment of Innocence and The Apple*', in Jinhee Choi and Mattias Frey (eds), *Cine-Ethics: Ethical Dimensions of Film Theory, Practice, and Spectatorship*, New York and London: Routledge, pp. 125–41.

Bolton, Lucy (2011) *Film and Female Consciousness: Irigaray, Cinema and Thinking Women*, London: Palgrave Macmillan.

Bourdieu, Pierre (1977), *Outline of a Theory of Practice*, Cambridge: Cambridge University Press.

Bradley, Peri (ed.) (2016), *Food, Media and Contemporary Culture*, Bournemouth: Palgrave.

Bruno, Giuliana (2002), *Atlas of Emotion: Journeys in Art, Architecture and Film*, New York: Verso.

Bruzzi, Stella (1997), *Undressing Cinema: Clothing and Identity at the Movies*, London and New York: Routledge.

Buckmaster, Luke (2015), 'The Last Days of Chez Nous rewatched – emotions laid bare with a steady, sympathetic hand', *The Guardian*, 26 July, <https://www.theguardian.com/film/2015/jul/26/the-last-days-of-chez-nous-rewatched-emotions-laid-bare-with-a-steady-sympathetic-hand> (last accessed 22 April 2020).

Burch, Noël (1990), 'Building a Haptic Space', *Life to Those Shadows*, Berkeley: University of California Press, pp. 162–85.

Cannes news footage (1979), property of National Film and Sound Archives.

Caputo, Raffaele (1992), 'The Last Days of Chez Nous: Gillian Armstrong Interviewed', *Cinema Papers*, 90 (October), pp. 4–8.

Carter, Helen (2019), *Cinematography in films directed by Gillian Armstrong*, unpublished PhD thesis, Flinders University, Adelaide, Australia.

Chanter, Tina (2001), 'Introduction', in Tina Chanter (ed.), *Feminist Interpretations of Emmanuel Levinas*, Pennsylvania: Penn State University Press.

Chapman, Jan (2003), 'Some Significant Women in Australian Film – a celebration and a cautionary tale', *Metro*, 136, pp. 98–107.

Christiensen, Christian (2009), 'Political Documentary, online organization, and activist synergies', *Studies in Documentary Film*, 3.2, pp. 77–94.

Clover, Carol (1992), *Men, Women, and Chainsaws: Gender and the Modern Horror Film*, Brunswick, NJ: Princeton University Press.

Cobb, Shelley (2015), *Adaptation, Authorship, and Contemporary Women Filmmakers*, London: Palgrave.

Collins, Felicity (1999), *The Films of Gillian Armstrong*, St. Kilda: Atom.

Collins, Felicity and Therese Davis (2004), *Australian Cinema after* Mabo, Cambridge: Cambridge University Press.

Connolly, Keith (1981), 'Australia's Pride is its "New Wave" of Films', *New York Times*, 15 February.

Craven, Ian (ed.) (2001), *Australian Cinema in the 1990s*, London: Frank Cass.

Cunningham, Stuart (1985), 'Hollywood genres, Australian movies', in Albert Moran and Tom O'Regan (eds), *An Australian Film Reader*, Sydney: Currency Press, pp. 235–41.

Cunningham, Stuart (2009), *In the Vernacular: A Generation of Australian Culture and Controversy*, Brisbane: University of Queensland Press.

D'Erasmo, Stacey (2002), 'Northern Exposures', *New York Times*, April 21, p. 8, <https://www.nytimes.com/2002/04/21/books/northern-exposures.html> (last accessed 22 April 2020).

Davis, Therese (2004), *The Face on Screen: Death, Recognition & Spectatorship*, Bristol: Intellect.

Davis, Therese (2014), 'Locating *The Sapphires*: transnational and cross-cultural dimensions of an Australian Indigenous musical film', *Continuum: Journal of Media & Cultural Studies*, 28.5, pp. 594–604, <https://doi-org.ezproxy.flinders.edu.au/10.1080/10304312.2014.941972> (last accessed 17 April 2020).

Davis, Therese and Belinda Smaill (2014), 'Introduction: The Place of the Contemporary Female Director', *Camera Obscura*, 29.1 (85), pp. 1–3.

De Lauretis, Teresa (1983), *Alice Doesn't: Feminism, Semiotics, Cinema*, Bloomington: Indiana University Press.

De Lauretis, Teresa (1994), *The Practice of Love: Lesbian Sexuality and Perverse Desire*, Bloomington: Indiana University Press.

Del Río, Elena (2014), *Deleuze and the Cinemas of Performance*, Edinburgh: Edinburgh University Press.

Dermody, Susan and Elizabeth Jacka (1988), *The Screening of Australia: Anatomy of a National Cinema, volume 2*, Sydney: Currency Press.

Desser, David (2012), 'Global Noir: Genre Film in the Age of Transnationalism', in Barry Keith Grant (ed.), *Film Genre Reader IV*, Austin: University of Texas Press, pp. 628–48.

Devlin-Glass, Frances (2011), 'En-gendering the nation: Gender-bending and nationalism in Miles Franklin's "My Brilliant Career" and Emily Lawless's "Grania: The story of an island"', *Australasian Journal of Irish Studies*, 11, pp. 73–85.

Dibeltulo, Silvia and Ciara Barrett (2018), 'Introduction', in Dibeltulo and Barrett (eds), *Rethinking Genre in Contemporary Global Cinema*, Cham, Switzerland: Palgrave Macmillan, pp. 1–11.

Doane, Mary Ann (1987), *The Desire to Desire: The Woman's Film of the 1940s*, Bloomington: Indiana University Press.

Doane, Mary Ann (2003), 'The Close-Up: Scale and Detail in Cinema' *Differences: A Journal of Feminist Cultural Studies*, 14.3 (Fall), pp. 89–111.

Donald, Ella (2017), 'Her Brilliant Career: Gillian Armstrong on the Australian Screen Then and Now', *Metro*, 194, pp. 108–13.

Douglas, James Robert (2016), 'Gillian Armstrong: I used to think, "I did it, why can't all the other women?"', *The Guardian*, 30 August, <https://www.theguardian.com/film/2016/aug/30/gillian-armstrong-i-used-to-think-i-did-it-why-cant-all-the-other-women> (last accessed 22 April 2020).

Downing, Lisa and Libby Saxton (2010), *Film and Ethics: Foreclosed Encounters*, Oxford: Routledge.

Dyer, Richard (1982), 'Don't Look Now: the male pin-up', *Screen* 23.3–4 (Sept/Oct 1982), pp. 61–73, https://doi.org/10.1093/screen/23.3-4.61 (last accessed 22 April 2020).

Ebert, Roger (1984), 'Mrs. Soffel', RogerEbert.com, 1 January, <https://www.rogerebert.com/reviews/mrs-soffel-1984> (last accessed 22 April 2020).

Ebert, Roger (1993) *The Last Days of Chez Nous* review, RogerEbert.com, 16 April, <https://www.rogerebert.com/reviews/the-last-days-of-chez-nous-1993> (last accessed 22 April 2020).

Ebert, Roger (2002), *Charlotte Gray* review, RogerEbert.com, 11 January, <https://www.rogerebert.com/reviews/charlotte-gray-2002> (last accessed 22 April 2020).

Ebiri, Bilge (2016), 'Gillian Armstrong, One of Our Greatest Directors, on the Genius of Costumers', *The Village Voice*, 17 August, <https://www.villagevoice.com/2016/08/17/gillian-armstrong-one-of-our-great-directors-on-the-genius-of-costumers/> (last accessed 22 April 2020).

Eden, Allison, Serena Daalmans, Merel Van Ommen, and Addy Weljers (2017), 'Melfi's Choice: Morally Conflicted Content Leads to Moral Rumination in Viewers', *Journal of Media Ethics*, 32.3, pp. 142–53.

Edwards, Russell (2006), '*Unfolding Florence: The Many Lives of Florence Broadhurst*', *Variety*, 402.2, p. 40.

Elliott, Bonnie (2010), 'Period', in Ben Goldsmith and Geoff Leland (eds), *Directory of World Cinema: Australia and New Zealand*, Bristol: Intellect, pp. 146–50.

Elsaesser, Thomas and Malte Hagener (2010), *Film Theory: An Introduction through the Senses*, New York: Routledge.

Enker, Debi (1985), 'Coming in from the cold', *Cinema Papers*, 52 (July), p. 27.

Erhart, Julia (2018), *Gendering History on Screen: Women Filmmakers and Historical Films*, London: IB Tauris.

Errigo, Angie (2000), '*Charlotte Gray* Review', *Empire online*, 1 January, <https://www.empireonline.com/movies/charlotte-gray/review/> (last accessed 22 April 2020).

Ezra, Elizabeth and Terry Rowden (2006), 'General Introduction: What Is Transnational Cinema?', in Elizabeth Ezra and Terry Rowden (eds), *Transnational Cinema: The Film Reader*, London: Routledge, pp. 1–12.

Feuer, Jane (2012), 'The Self-Reflexive Musical and the Myth of Entertainment', in Barry Keith Grant (ed.), *Film Genre Reader IV*, Austin: University of Texas Press, pp. 543–57.

Franklin, Miles [1901] (1980), *My Brilliant Career*, London: Virago.

Freedman, Adele (1980), 'Sybylla's just a girl who can't say yes', *The Globe and Mail*, Toronto, 12 July, p. E3.

French, Lisa (2014), 'The international reception of Australian women filmmakers', *Continuum, Journal of Media & Cultural Studies*, 28.5 (August), pp. 654–65.

French, Lisa (2018), 'Women in the Director's Chair: The "Female Gaze" in Documentary Film", in Boel Ulfsdotter and Anna Backman Rogers (eds), *Female Authorship and the Documentary Image: Theory, Practice and Aesthetics*, Edinburgh: Edinburgh University Press, pp. 9–21.

Gaines, Jane (2018), *Pink-Slipped: What Happened to Women in the Silent Film Industries?*, Urbana: University of Illinois Press.

Garcia, Desirée J. (2014), *The Migration of Musical Film: From Ethnic Margins to American Mainstream*, Brunswick, NJ: Rutgers.

Gerstner, David (2010), 'Christophe Honoré's *Les Chansons d'amour* and the Musical's Queer-abilities', in Steve Cohan (ed.), *The Sound of Musicals*, London: Palgrave, pp. 188–99.

'Gillian Armstrong on her crowdsourced doc *The Inspiring Story of Us*', Staff Writer, 27 January 2016, <https://www.if.com.au/gillian-

armstrong-on-her-crowdsourced-doc-the-inspiring-story-of-us/> (last accessed 1 November 2019).

Ginsberg, Faye (2002), 'Screen Memories: Resignifying the Traditional in Indigenous Media', in Ginsberg, Lila Abu-Lughod, and Brian Larkin (eds), *Media Worlds: Anthropology on New Terrain*, Berkeley: University of California Press.

Goldsmith, Ben (2010), 'Outward-Looking Australian Cinema', *Studies in Australasian Cinema*, 4.3, pp. 199–214. Cited in Adrian Danks, Stephen Gaunson, Peter C. Kunze (eds) (2018), *American-Australian Cinema: Transnational Connections*, Cham, Switzerland: Palgrave Macmillan.

Goodall, Heather and Allison Cadzow (2009), *Rivers and Resilience: Aboriginal People on Sydney's George's River*, Sydney: University of New South Wales Press.

Green, Susan (2007), '*Unfolding Florence: The Many Lives of Florence Broadhurst*', *Boxoffice*, 143.5, p. 73.

Grønstad, Asbjørn (2012), *Screening the Unwatchable: Spaces of Negation in Post-Millennial Art Cinema*, Basingstoke and New York: Palgrave Macmillan.

Grosz, Elizabeth (1995), *Space, Time and Perversion*, New York and London: Routledge.

Gunning, Tom (2015), 'Phantom Images and Modern Manifestations: Spirit Photography, Magic Theater, Trick Films, and Photography's Uncanny', in Murray Leeder, Jeffrey Sconce (eds), *Cinematic Ghosts: Haunting and Spectrality from Silent Cinema to the Digital Era*, London: Bloomsbury Press, pp. 17–38.

Gunning, Tom (2018), 'The Impossible Body of Early Film', in Marina Dahlquiest, Doron Galili, Jan Olsson, and Valentine Robert (eds), *Corporeality in Early Cinema: Viscera, Skin, and Physical Form*, Bloomington: Indiana University Press, pp. 13–24.

Gustafsson, Tommy and Pietari, Kääpä (2015), *Nordic Genre Film: Small National Film Cultures in the Global Marketplace*, Edinburgh: Edinburgh University Press.

Hall, Sarah (2017), 'Director Gillian Armstrong: some notes on a brilliant career', *Precinct*, Melbourne, 11 August, <https://precinct.finearts-music.unimelb.edu.au/2017/08/11/director-gillian-armstrong-some-notes-on-a-brilliant-career/> (last accessed 23 April 2020).

Harrod, Mary and Katarzyna Paszkiewicz (2018), 'Introduction', in Mary Harrod and Katarzyna Paszkiewicz (eds), *Women Do Genre in Film and Television*, New York: Routledge, pp. 1–20.

Hastie, Amelie (2007), *Cupboards of Curiosity: Women, Recollection, and Film History*, Chapel Hill, NC: Duke University Press.

Hershey, Megan and Michael Artime (2014), 'Narratives of Africa in a Digital World: Kony 2012 and Student Perceptions of Conflict and Agency in Sub-Saharan Africa', *PS: Political Science & Politics*, 47.3, pp. 636–41.

Highmore, Ben (2010), 'Bitter after Taste: Affect, Food, and Social Aesthetics', in Melissa Gregg and Gregory J. Seigworth (eds), *The Affect Theory Reader*, Durham, NC: Duke University Press, pp. 118–37.

Higson, Andrew (2006), 'The Limiting Imagination of National Cinema', in Elizabeth Ezra and Terry Rowden (eds), *Transnational Cinema: The Film Reader*, London: Routledge, pp. 15–25.

Hogan, Christine (1982), 'New Directions for Gillian Armstrong', *Australian Women's Weekly*, 26 May, p. 62.

Holden, Stephen (2001), 'Film review; She Does What She Must for Her Cause', *New York Times*, 28 December, <https://www.nytimes.com/2001/12/28/movies/film-review-she-does-what-she-must-for-her-cause.html> (last accessed 23 April 2020).

Hole, Kristin (2016), *Towards a Feminist Cinematic Ethics; Claire Denis, Emmanuel Levinas and Jean-Luc Nancy*, Edinburgh: Edinburgh University Press.

Hooks, Barbara (1998), 'Armstrong comes full circle', *The Age*, 18 June, p. 3.

Hustvedt, Asti (2011), *Media Muses: Hysteria in Nineteenth Century Paris*, New York: Norton.

Ireland, Haidee (2013), 'The case of Agnes Jones: tracing Aboriginal presence in Sydney through criminal justice records', *History Australia*, 10.3, pp. 236–51.

Jameson, Fredric (1982), *The Political Unconscious: Narration as a Socially Symbolic Act*, Ithaca: Cornell University Press.

Jermyn, Deborah (2018), 'The Contemptible Realm of the Romcom Queen: Nancy Meyers, Cultural Value and Romantic Comedy', in Mary Harrod and Katarzyna Paszkiewicz (eds), *Women Do Genre in Film and Television*, London: Routledge, pp. 57–71.

Johnson, Anthony (2014), 'Explainer: what does a film producer do?', *The Conversation*, 10 April, https://theconversation.com/explainer-what-does-a-film-producer-do-22173 (last accessed 23 April 2020).

Karskens, Grace (2009), *The Colony*, Crows Nest, NSW: Allen & Unwin.

Kavenagh, Terence (2009), 'Distant Echoes: Aboriginal and Islander boys at St. Mary's Sydney in the mid-nineteenth century', *Tjurunga*, 76 (May), pp. 60–96.

Kelly, Paula (2011), 'Morality and the Law in "Cunnamulla"', *Metro Magazine: Media & Education Magazine*, 168, pp. 84–8.

Koivunen, Anu (2015), 'The Promise of Touch: Turns to Affect in Feminist Film Theory', in Laura Mulvey and Anna Backman Rogers (eds),

Feminisms: Diversity, Difference and Multiplicity in Contemporary Film Cultures, Amsterdam: Amsterdam University Press, pp. 97–110.

Krakowiak, Maja and Mary Beth Oliver (2012), 'When Good Characters Do Bad Things: Examining the Effect of Moral Ambiguity on Enjoyment', *Journal of Communication*, 62, pp. 117–35.

Kupfer, Joseph H. (2012), *Feminist Ethics in Film: Feminist Ethics in Film: Reconfiguring Care Through Cinema*, Chicago: Intellect.

Laffly, Tomris (2016), 'Gillian Armstrong: "Film is not a level playing field for women"', *Film School Rejects*, 9 August, <https://filmschoolrejects.com/gillian-armstrong-film-is-not-a-level-playing-field-for-women-b19cd-21f3ee1/> (last accessed 23 April 2020).

Levinas, Emmanuel (1989), 'Ethics as First Philosophy' in Sean Hand (ed.), *The Levinas Reader*, Oxford: Basil Blackwell.

Levy, Emanuel (1997), 'Oscar and Lucinda', *Variety*, 6 December, <https://variety.com/1997/film/reviews/oscar-and-lucinda-111738170/> (last accessed 23 April 2020).

McComb, Samuel (1910), 'Nervousness – A National Menace', *Everybody's Magazine*, 22, pp. 259–60.

McFarlane, Brian (2008), 'Her Brilliant Career: Gillian Armstrong on Four Decades of Filmmaking', *Metro*, 156, pp. 16–21.

MacKenzie, Scott (ed.) (2014), *Film Manifestos and Global Cinema Cultures*, Berkeley: University of California Press.

Magarey, Susan (2002), '*My Brilliant Career* and Feminism', *Australian Literary Studies*, 20.4, pp. 389–98.

Marks, Laura (2002), *Touch: Sensuous Theory and Multisensorial Media*, Minneapolis: University of Minnesota Press.

Marshall, Alan [1949] (1972), *How Beautiful Are Thy Feet*, Melbourne, VIC: First Gold Star paperbound edition (first published by The Chesterhill Press).

Marshall, Alan (1977), 'Old Mrs. Bilson', in *The Complete Stories of Alan Marshall*, West Melbourne, VIC: Thomas Nelson, pp. 411–22.

Mathews, Sue (1984), *35mm Dreams: Conversations with Five Directors About the Australian Film Revival*, Ringwood, VIC: Penguin.

Mayne, Judith (1994), *Directed by Dorothy Arzner*, Bloomington: Indiana University Press.

Miller, Jacqui (2013), *Film and Ethics: What Would You Have Done?*, Newcastle upon Tyne: Cambridge Scholars Publishing.

Moran, Albert and Errol Vieth (2006), *Film in Australia: An Introduction*, Cambridge: Cambridge University Press.

Mordue, Mark (1989), 'Homeward Bound', *Sight and Sound*, 58.4 (Autumn), pp. 270–2.

Mordue, Mark (1992), 'The Feminine Mystique', *Rolling Stone* (October), pp. 63–5.

Moritz, William [1996] (2012), 'Some Critical Perspectives on Lotte Reiniger', in Maureen Furniss (ed.), *Animation: Art & Industry*, New Barnet: John Libbey Publishing, pp. 13–19.

Mulvey, Laura (1990), 'Visual Pleasure and Narrative Cinema', *Screen*, 16.3 (Autumn 1975), reprinted in Patricia Erens (ed.) (1990), *Issues in Feminist Film Criticism*, Bloomington: Indiana University Press, pp. 28–40.

Nannicelli, Ted (2006), 'From Representation to Evocation: Tracing a Progression in Jean Rouch's *Les magiciens de Wanzerbé, Les maîtres fous*, and *Jaguar*', *Visual Anthropology*, 19.2, pp. 123–43.

Neale, Steve (2012), 'Questions of Genre', in Barry Keith Grant (ed.), *Film Genre Reader IV*, Austin: University of Texas Press, pp. 178–202.

Negra, Diana and Su Holmes (2011), *In the Limelight and Under the Microscope: Forms and Functions of Female Celebrity*, New York: Continuum.

Neill, Alex (2006), 'Empathy and (Film) Fiction', in Noel Carroll and Jinhee Choi (eds), *Philosophy of Film and Motion Pictures: An Anthology*, Malden and Oxford: Blackwell.

Neill, Rosemary (1988), 'Her Brilliant Career, Gillian Armstrong Film Director', *The Bulletin*, 30 August, pp. 141–4.

Nichols, Bill (1992), *Representing Reality: Issues and Concepts in Documentary*, Bloomington: Indiana University Press.

Nichols, Bill (2016), *Speaking Truths with Film: Evidence, Ethics, Politics in Documentary*, Berkeley: University of California Press.

Nichols, Bill (2017), *Introduction to Documentary* (3rd edn), Bloomington: Indiana University Press.

Nielsen, Kim E. (2019), 'Dr. Anna B. Ott, Patient #1763: The Messiness of Authority, Diagnosis, Gender, and Insanity in Nineteenth Century America', *Signs*, 45.1, pp. 27–49.

O'Grady, Sue Ellen (1979), 'Gillian Armstrong: Directing Her Own Brilliant Career', *Cleo* (May), pp. 62–7.

O'Malley, Sheila (2019), 'The Nightingale', RogerEbert.com, 2 August, <https://www.rogerebert.com/reviews/the-nightingale-2019> (last accessed 27 April 2020).

Oliete-Aldea, Elena, Beatriz Oria, Juan A. Tarancón (2015), *Global Genres, Local Films: The Transnational Dimension of Spanish Cinema*, Oxford: Bloomsbury.

Osmond, Gary (2017), 'Indigenous sporting pasts: resuscitating Aboriginal swimming history', *Australian Aboriginal Studies*, 2, pp. 43–55.

Parpart, Lee (2010), 'Feminist Ambiguity in the film adaptations of Lynne Stopkewich', in Brenda Austin-Smith and George Melnyk (eds), *The Gendered Screen: Canadian Women Filmmakers*, Waterloo, ON: Wilfrid Laurier University Press.

Paszkiewicz, Katarzyna (2018), *Genre, Authorship and Contemporary Women Filmmakers*, Edinburgh: Edinburgh University Press.

Peach, Ricardo (2005), '"The Wolf is After Your Basket!" A Brief History of Australian Queer Cinematic Cultures', in *Queer Cinema as Fifth Cinema in South Africa and Australia*, PhD Thesis, University of Technology Sydney.

Pidduck, Julianne (2004), *Contemporary Costume Film: Space, Place and the Past*, London: British Film Institute.

Plantinga, Carl (1999), 'The Scene of Empathy and the Human Face on Film', in Plantinga and Greg M. Smith (eds), *Passionate Views: Film, Cognition, and Emotion*, Baltimore: The Johns Hopkins University Press, pp. 239–55.

Polaschek, Bronwyn (2013), *The Postfeminist Biopic: Narrating the Lives of Plath, Kahlo, Woolf and Austen*, Basingstoke: Palgrave Macmillan.

Porter, Hal (1963), 'Gretel', *The Literary Review*, 7.2, pp. 233–46.

Projansky, Sarah (2014), *Spectacular Girls: Media Fascination and Celebrity Culture*, New York: New York University Press.

Quinn, Karl (2014), 'Why Won't We Watch Australian Films?', *The Sydney Morning Herald*, 26 October, <https://www.smh.com.au/entertainment/movies/why-wont-we-watch-australian-films-20141024-11bhia.html> (last accessed 27 April 2020).

Quinn, Karl (2017), 'Gillian Armstrong lends her voice to campaign to save Australian screen content', *The Sydney Morning Herald*, 17 September, <http://www.smh.com.au/entertainment/movies/gillian-armstrong-lends-her-voice-to-campaign-to-save-australian-screen-content-20170917-gyj16x.html> (last accessed 27 April 2020).

Radway, Janice (1984), *Reading the Romance: Women, Patriarchy, and Popular Literature*, Chapel Hill: University of North Carolina Press.

Raj, Hari (2015), 'Her Brilliant Career: Hari Raj Meets Gillian Armstrong', *The Weekly Review*, 19–25 August, pp. 10–11, <https://issuu.com/theweeklyreview.com.au/docs/bay-bayside-20150819-iss> (last accessed 1 May 2020).

Raynor, Jonathan (2000), *Contemporary Australian Cinema: An Introduction*, Manchester: Manchester University Press.

Reichl, Ruth (1995), 'At Tea With Gillian Armstrong: A Lucky Director's Daring Career', *The New York Times*, 8 March, B1–B2.

Reid, Mary Anne (1999), *More Long Shots: Australian Cinema Successes in the 90s*, Sydney: Australian Film Commission.

Rich, Ruby (1998), *Chick Flicks: Theories and Memories of the Feminist Film Movement*, Durham, NC: Duke University Press.

Robson, Naomi (1997), Interview with Armstrong, *Today Tonight* with Naomi Robson. Property of National Film and Sound Archive.

Rosenfeld, Megan (1983), 'Gillian Armstrong: The Free Spirit Rides a New Wave', *The Washington Post*, 15 April, https://www.washingtonpost.com/archive/lifestyle/1983/04/15/gillian-armstrong-the-free-spirit-

rides-a-new-wave/83b0b54d-172c-4406-98cd-80a272ea28f1/?utm_
term=.8be2f4dd8d87 (last accessed 1 May 2020).

Ross, Karen (2009), *Gendered Media: Women, Men, and Identity Politics*,
Lanham, MD: Rowman & Littlefield.

Rueschmann, Eva (2000), *Sisters on Screen: Siblings in Contemporary Cinema*,
Philadelphia: Temple University Press.

Ryan, Mark David (2010), 'Towards an understanding of Australian genre
cinema and entertainment: Beyond the limitations of "Ozploitation"
discourse', *Continuum: Journal of Media & Cultural Studies*, 24.6,
pp. 843–54.

Ryan, Mark David (2012), 'A silver bullet for Australian cinema? Genre movies
and the audience debate', *Studies in Australasian cinema*, 6.2, pp. 141–57.

Ryan, Mark David and Ben Goldsmith (2017), 'Australian Screen in the 2000s:
An Introduction', in Mark David Ryan and Ben Goldsmith (eds), *Australian
Screen in the 2000s*, London: Palgrave, pp. 1–21.

Ryan, Tom (1980), 'Historical Films', in Scott Murray (ed.), *The New Australian
Cinema*, West Melbourne, VIC: Nelson, pp. 113–31.

Savigny, Heather and Helen Warner (eds) (2015), *The Politics of Being a
woman: Feminism, Media and 21st Century Popular Culture*, Basingstoke:
Palgrave Macmillan.

Saxton, Libby (2008), *Haunted Images: Film, Ethics, Testimony and the
Holocaust*, London and New York: Wallflower Press.

Schembri, Jim (1996), 'Armstrong's New Generation', *The Age*, 17 July,
pp. 12–13.

Scott, A.O. (2019), '"The Nightingale" Review: A Song of Violence
and Vengeance', *New York Times*, 1 August, https://www.nytimes
.com/2019/08/01/movies/nightingale-review.html (last accessed 1
May 2020).

Scott, Jay (1979), 'Picnic at Hanging Rock fails to serve main course', *The Globe
and Mail*, Toronto, 31 March, p. 35.

Screen Australia website, <https://www.screenaustralia.gov.au/fact-finders/
production-trends/feature-production/all-feature-films/budget-ranges>
(last accessed 1 May 2020).

Shaw, Deborah and Armida De La Garza (2010), 'Introducing Transnational
Cinemas', *Transnational Cinemas*, 1.1, pp. 3–6.

Shirley, Graham (2011), 'Gillian Armstrong, National Film and Sound
Archives, Oral History Interview', Canberra: National Film and Sound
Archives.

Shit People Say to Women Directors, <http://shitpeoplesaytowomendirec-
tors.tumblr.com/> (last accessed 1 May 2020).

Sinnerbrink, Robert (2016), *Cinematic Ethics: Exploring Ethical Experience
through Film*, London: Routledge.

Smaill, Belinda (2011), 'History, Feminism and Time: Gillian Armstrong's Documentary Series', *Metro*, 167, pp. 102–7.

Smith, Nathan (2014), 'The Adventures of *Priscilla, Queen of the Desert*: Why It Still Survives', *Out Magazine*, 10 October, <https://www.out.com/movies/2014/10/10/adventures-priscilla-queen-desert-why-it-still-survives> (last accessed 1 May 2020).

Sobchack, Vivienne (1992), *The Address of the Eye: A Phenomenology of Film Experience*, Princeton, NJ: Princeton University Press.

Sobchack, Vivienne (2004), *Carnal Thoughts: Embodiment and Moving Image Culture*, Berkeley, Los Angeles and London: University of California Press.

Stadler, Jane (2014), 'Cinema's Compassionate Gaze: Empathy, Affect, and Aesthetics in The Diving Bell and the Butterfly', in Jinhee Choi and Mattias Frey (eds), *Cine-Ethics: Ethical Dimensions of Film Theory, Practice, and Spectatorship*, New York: Routledge, pp. 27–42.

Stamp, Shelley (2015), *Lois Weber in early Hollywood*, Berkeley: University of California Press.

Surkis, Judith (n.d.), 'Alice Winocour's *Augustine*', in Fiction and Film for Scholars of France: A Cultural Bulletin, <https://h-france.net/fffh/the-buzz/alice-winocours-augustine/> (last accessed 1 May 2020).

Tashiro, Charles (1998), *Pretty Pictures: Production Design and the History Film*, Austin: University of Texas Press.

Tasker, Yvonne (2010), 'Vision and Visibility: Women Filmmakers, Contemporary Authorship, and Feminist Film Studies', in Vicki Callahan (ed.), *Reclaiming the Archive: Feminism and Film History*, Detroit: Wayne State University Press.

Taylor, Anthea (2014), 'Germain Greer's Adaptable Celebrity: Feminism, Unruliness, and Humour on the British Small Screen', *Feminist Media Studies*, 14.5, pp. 759–74.

Taylor, Craig (2011), 'Literature, Moral Reflection and Ambiguity', *Philosophy*, 86.1, pp. 75–93.

Taylor, Ella (1995), 'Creating Havoc in Hollywood', *New Woman*, July, pp. 78–83.

Teays, Wanda (2012), *Seeing the Light: Exploring Ethics through Movies*, Malden, MA: Wiley-Blackwell.

Thompson, Peter (1983), 'Filmmaker Interview: Gillian Armstrong', copyright AFTS, 15 June.

Thomson-Jones, Katherine (2008), *Aesthetics and Film*, London and New York: Continuum.

Thornham, Sue (2012), *What if I Had Been the Hero?: Investigating Women's Cinema*, London: British Film Institute.

Thornham, Sue (2019), *Spaces of Women's Cinema: Space, Place and Genre in Contemporary Women's Filmmaking*, London: British Film Institute.

Tomsic, Mary (2017), *Beyond the Silver Screen: A History of Women, Filmmaking and Film Culture in Australia 1920–1990*, Melbourne: Melbourne University Press.

Travers, Peter (1993), *The Last Days of Chez Nous* review, *Rolling Stone*, 26 February, <https://www.rollingstone.com/movies/movie-reviews/the-last-days-of-chez-nous-251782/> (last accessed 1 May 2020).

Tripp, Amber (2010), 'Tracee Hutchison, Gillian Armstrong and Shirley Shackleton', *ABC Radio*, 7 May, Melbourne, <http://www.abc.net.au/local/audio/2010/05/07/2893588.htm> (last accessed 1 May 2020).

Tsaliki, Lisa (2016), '"Tweeting the Good Causes": social networking and celebrity activism', in P. David Marshall and Sean Redmond (eds), *A Companion to Celebrity*, Hoboken, NJ: Wiley, pp. 235–57.

Tsang, Tiffany Lee (2015), '"A Fair Chance for the Girls": Discourse on Women's Health and Higher Education in Late Nineteenth Century America', *American Educational History Journal*, 42.2, pp. 137–50.

Turner, Graeme (1989), 'Art Directing History: The Period Film', in Albert Moran and Tom O'Regan (eds), *The Australian Screen*, Ringwood, VIC: Penguin, pp. 99–117.

Turner, Graeme (2004), *Understanding Celebrity*, London: Sage.

Ulfsdotter, Boel and Anna Backman Rogers (eds) (2018), *Female Authorship and the Documentary Image: Theory, Practice and Aesthetics*, Edinburgh: Edinburgh University Press.

Velasco, Carlos, Yunwen Tu, Marianna Obrist (2018), 'Towards Multisensory Storytelling with Taste and Flavor', Conference Proceedings ICMI (International Conference on Multimodal Interaction), Boulder, CO, <https://doi.org/10.1145/3279954.3279956> (last accessed 1 May 2020).

Vidal, Belén (2012), *Figuring the Past: Period Film and the Mannerist Aesthetic*, Amsterdam: Amsterdam University Press.

Weinstein, Anna (2013), 'Spotlight on Gillian Armstrong', *Film International*, 11.2, pp. 89–91.

White, David (1984), *Australian Movies to the World: The International Success of Australian Films since 1970*, Sydney and Melbourne: Fontana and Cinema Papers.

White, Patricia (2015), *Women's Cinema, World Cinema: Projecting Contemporary Feminisms*, Durham, NC: Duke University Press.

Whitley, Claire (2018), *Gender and Comedy after Bridesmaids: The Womance Comedy*, PhD thesis (under construction), Flinders University, Adelaide, Australia.

Wicke, Jennifer (1994), 'Celebrity Feminism: Materialist Feminism and the Culture of Celebrity', *South Atlantic Quarterly*, 93.4, pp. 751–78.

Williams, Linda (2000), 'Film Bodies: Gender, Genre, Excess', in Robert Stam and Toby Miller (eds), *Film and Theory: An Anthology*, Malden, MA: Blackwell, pp. 207–21.

Williamson, Kirstin (1979), 'Gillian's Brilliant Career', *National Times*, 6 October, p. 19.

Wood, Gary (1998), 'My Brilliant Career Down Under in Film and Television', *New Statesman*, 27 March, 11.497, pp. 44–5.

Worthy, Blythe (2017), 'Questioning the "Strong Female Character": Gillian Armstrong's *High Tide* (1987)', *Senses of Cinema*, 83 (July), <http://sensesofcinema.com/2017/pioneering-australian-women/high-tide-1987/> (last accessed 1 May 2020).

Zecchi, Barbara (2018), 'Comedy as a Feminist Strategy: Spanish Women Filmmakers Reclaim Laughter', trans. Mary Harrod and Katarzyna Paszkiewicz, in Mary Harrod and Katarzyna Paszkiewicz (eds), *Women Do Genre in Film and Television*, New York: Routledge, pp. 91–105.

Index

Printed and bound by CPI Group (UK) Ltd, Croydon, CR0 4YY

21/01/2025

01823455-0001